国际和平城市
丛书

International Cities
of Peace

国家出版基金项目
江苏省"十四五"重点图书出版规划项目
侵华日军南京大屠杀遇难同胞纪念馆资助项目

中国
南京

NANJING

China

International Cities of Peace

Series Editor: Liu Cheng
Associate Editors: Ling Xi　Chen Junfeng

Academic Advisor: Liu Cheng

Bai Shuang　**Translated by Fan Haixiang**

南京师范大学出版社

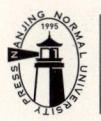

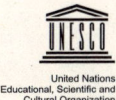

United Nations Educational, Scientific and Cultural Organization

UNESCO Chair on Peace Studies
Nanjing University
People's Republic of China

图书在版编目(CIP)数据

中国·南京 = Nanjing, China：英文 / 白爽著；范海祥译 . -- 南京：南京师范大学出版社，2022.8
（国际和平城市丛书 / 刘成主编）
ISBN 978-7-5651-5350-1

Ⅰ. ①中… Ⅱ. ①白… ②范… Ⅲ. ①南京—概况—英文 Ⅳ. ①K925.31

中国版本图书馆 CIP 数据核字 (2022) 第 111524 号

丛 书 名	国际和平城市丛书
丛书主编	刘 成
丛书副主编	凌 曦　陈俊峰
书　　名	Nanjing, China
学术顾问	刘 成
著　　者	白 爽
译　　者	范海祥
策划编辑	徐 蕾　郑海燕
责任编辑	王雅琼
书籍设计	瀚清堂
出版发行	南京师范大学出版社
地　　址	江苏省南京市玄武区后宰门西村 9 号（邮编：210016）
电　　话	(025)83598712（编辑部）83598919（总编办）83598412（营销部）
网　　址	http://press.njnu.edu.cn
电子信箱	nspzbb@njnu.edu.cn
照　　排	南京私书坊文化传播有限公司
印　　刷	上海雅昌艺术印刷有限公司
开　　本	889 毫米 ×1194 毫米　1/32
印　　张	8.75
版　　次	2022 年 8 月第 1 版　2022 年 8 月第 1 次印刷
书　　号	ISBN 978-7-5651-5350-1
定　　价	50.00 元
出 版 人	张志刚

* 南京师大版图书若有印装问题请与销售商调换
* 版权所有　侵权必究

Foreword by Series Editor

This book series, International Cities of Peace, Volume I, introduces five cities, which have one thing in common that they have all experienced the trauma of war in their history, and the collective memories have endured from one generation to the next. So, history must be kept in mind. Only by looking back on past sufferings and using history as a mirror can we prevent such historical tragedies from occurring again. It is absolutely vital to recognize and remember the historical trauma, but how we remember it may affect its authenticity and how long we will keep it in mind. According to history, building peace is the best remedy for remembering and recovering from the past suffering. When the traumatic memory of a city is transformed into a common human memory, we can understand the past disasters in a new way beyond stereotyped political memory. Only this can enable the traumatic history to be linked to the future peace, which can promote the reconciliation between the former hostile parties, and boost hope to the establishment of a community with a shared future for mankind. History indicates that reconciliation means not only exchanging our views and experiences of the past, but also a process of mutually creating new ideas for the future and sharing new experiences. In this way, reconciliation is a thought and a power that meets our mutual needs, which can be developed by building cities of peace with the legacy bequeathed by the war. That is why we wrote these books.

All the five cities of the book series are actively engaged in building a culture of peace. Nanjing, the first International City of Peace in China, held an international peace forum on positive peace; Dresden reflects on the war experience of Germany and strengthens domestic and international reconciliation; Hiroshima leads non-governmentally the anti-nuclear peace movement in Japan; Warsaw promotes the reconciliation dialogue that has led to a shared historical memory both inside and outside Poland; Coventry is the benchmark for British reconciliation. At the same time, the study of war memory is undergoing changes in three dimensions: shifts from the hero memory to the traumatic memory, from the memory of a victorious country to the memory of all the wounded countries, and from the domestic historical memory of a country to historical memory shared by many countries. Our belief is that the memory of war will be ultimately eclipsed by the memory of peace, as more and more cities work towards building cities of peace and thus form a global network of peace cities.

The five cities have their own characteristics in building a city of peace. Their practice of building peace has proven the truth that "There is no way to peace; peace is the way". Cities of peace all share a common purpose, promoting the culture of peace advocated by UNESCO, that is, working to build peace through conflict prevention, mediation and transformation; providing peace education on non-violence, tolerance, acceptance, respect and sustainable development; promoting intercultural dialogue and reconciliation. To build a city of peace requires the joint efforts of governments, universities, social groups, non-government organizations and citizens from all countries and regions around the world, for it needs to incorporate elements of peace in historical records, memories and heritage. It can be achieved in many ways, such as conflict prevention, peace-keeping, peace-building, peace research, peace education, and all peace activities that promote urban progress and prosperity as well as world peace and development.

This book series rests on its disciplinary foundation, Peace Studies. With the only UNESCO Chair on Peace Studies in China, Nanjing University is widely recognized as the center of China's Peace Studies. The development of China's Peace Studies has received great help from many institutions and individuals around the world. Without their support, Peace Studies would not have developed in China, and these books would not have been published, either. This book series took ten years to compile, experiencing ups and downs along the way, and finally came out. All the authors, translators and editors have done their best to bring out these books against all the odds, and make them authentic, scholarly, innovative, and readable at the same time.

This book series is an attempt to understand how cultural trauma and historical memory affect us. We sincerely welcome readers to point out and correct the defects and mistakes in these books.

Liu Cheng
Professor, School of History, Nanjing University
Chairholder of UNESCO Chair on Peace Studies
August 2022

Contents

001

Foreword by Series Editor

006

Introduction

008

Chapter 1	**Peace Born of the History**	
	Nanjing, the Ancient Capital	016
	Tangible Memory of Peace	031
	The Urban Character	050

074

Chapter 2	**Defending Peace against Atrocities**	
	Resistance in the Dark	079
	The Light of Peace in the Wartime	089
	The Hard-Fought Victory	110

118

Chapter 3	**Calling for Peace**	
	The City Bearing Scars	123
	Reshaping the Memory	138
	Pursuit of the Historical Truth	148

Chapter 4 Another Choice for Peace

Initiating Peace Studies in China	188
Practicing Peace Education in Nanjing	200
Peace-Oriented Transformation of Memorial Venues	212

Chapter 5 Continuing Peace-Building in the Future

A Peace-Loving Nation	230
Actions beyond Words	235
Collected Wisdom for Peace	252
An Ongoing Process	261

Conclusion

Main Bibliography

Afterword

Introduction

Nanjing is an ancient city and a special one. It has a refulgent history of a few thousand years in China as the "ancient capital of the Six Dynasties" and "the capital of Ten Regimes". Meanwhile, it is known as one of the world's four martyred cities during World War II, along with Coventry in the UK, Dresden in Germany, and Hiroshima in Japan. On December 13, 1937, the Japanese invaders captured the city and launched the Nanjing Massacre, which shocked China and foreign countries. The Chinese military and civilians fought back bravely, and got humanitarian assistance from international friends, who defended justice with their actions and even devoted their lives to protecting peace. The devastation of Nanjing after the war came to be a humiliation that the family and the country seemed indisposed to touch upon, and it also became the trauma in the memory of the Chinese nation.
For a long time, the nation was silently self-healing, and did not choose to apprise of nor show much of its tribulation to the outside world. It was not until the 1990s that this dark memory gradually began to attract more and more research attention and interests of dissemination. At present, only fifty odd survivors of the Nanjing Massacre are alive in the world. Therefore, it has become an urgent issue that how people understand and remember this painful experience, and prevent the tragedy of war from reoccurring, in the course of its urban development in the new era.

The miserable history must not be forgotten, while seeking peace is the best way of commemoration. Building sustainable peace is the vision of the entire world. There is an inscription of one single message in several languages on the stone wall at the entrance to the UNESCO headquarters, saying: "Since wars begin in the minds of men, it is in the minds of men that the defenses of peace must be constructed." Chinese President Xi Jinping pointed out in his speech at the UNESCO headquarters: "we must also step up cross-border, cross-time-and-space and cross-civilization activities in education, science, technology and culture to spread the seeds of the idea of peace far and wide, so that they will sprout, take root and grow in the hearts and minds of the world's people, and provide the planet we share with more and more forests of peace."

Nanjing has put various efforts on peace-building, which was reflected from its cultural heritage, its historical inheritance, and its civilians. On the premise of maintaining historical truth and justice, it has made the decision to build an international city of peace, and has transformed this historical memory into a force of maintaining peace, which reflects not only its responsibility, but also its unique development wisdom.

In Peace Studies, there is a very commonly used research method called "thinking beyond the wall". This book is supposed to open a new perspective to understand Nanjing, so that peace can be fully understood and practiced in it. Now the city has come slowly out of the shadow of history, and its future needs our generation to carry on. Though it may have many possibilities for its future, among them "peace" is supposed to be one of the key words. Nanjing will become the envoy of peace, sowing the seeds of peace from China to the rest of the world!

Chapter 1
Peace Born of the History

Nanjing is an ancient capital, a famous cultural city, and a city of peace.

This city has a unique natural beauty. Located in the center of the lower reaches of the Yangtze River, it is surrounded by mountains and has fertile land. Its superior topographical feature attracted many dynasties to establish their capital here, so it is known as the "ancient capital of the Six Dynasties" and "the capital of Ten Regimes".

Nanjing had different names in history, and "Jinling" was one of them. In 333 BC, King Chuwei built Jinling Town in the Stone City, hence the name of "Jinling" afterwards. In 229 AD, Sun Quan established the capital here. From then on, Nanjing has become the most renowned capital in the Yangtze River basin. The city, during the Six Dynasties period, also known as "Jiankang", was the first city in the world with a population of more than one million, and created the splendid "Six Dynasties Civilization". It is known as one of "the two centers of world classical civilization" together with ancient Rome.

When you saunter around the city, you may brush off the imprints of time, stroke the peace imprints of cultural and historical sites, and appreciate the poems and paintings of the literati. Seeing from the urban planning to the civilians' life, one can capture the feelings and character of the Nanjing residents, who love life and peace, and their innate inclusiveness and harmonious life, from a brick and a tile, a poem and a scene, a flower and a tree in every nook and cranny. All of these consist of the temperament, cultural atmosphere, and customs of this city.

Fig.1-1 *Guernica* by Pablo Picasso

However, Nanjing has suffered from the atrocities of war several times in history. It has gone through ups and downs time and time again, but still bursts from the ground like a tenacious seed in the sun. Every time it was reborn from Nirvana in the ruins of war, it became stronger and more unyielding, so it is fully aware of the preciousness of peace. Atrocities may happen again, but it has never

been an absolutely dominant factor, which is like the little flower in the center of Picasso's painting *Guernica* [Fig.1-1]. No matter how chaotic the external environment is, the renewed life that carries faith and peace will inevitably come to life.

Fig.1-2 **Nanjing Xuanwu Lake**

    Through the lens of history, we have discovered that the city is closely connected with peace. This connection is seen through its innate beauty of inclusiveness and harmony, as well as its urban temperament, cultural atmosphere and local customs. They represent and inherit the peace genes of the city, nurture people's love for peace and their infinite wisdom for peace.

The Legend of Goddess Nüwa Mending the Sky

In the ancient Chinese myth, there was a goddess, and her name was Nüwa. Long long ago when the sky was first separated from the earth, she began to create human beings with loess in imitation of herself, and a human society was built afterwards. However, the sky collapsed, so the goddess stepped forward, smelted the five-color stone to patch the hole in the roof and leveled the land to help the world's creatures from the catastrophe. There was also a saying that because there was not enough five-color stone for the mending, the goddess actually sacrificed her body to fill the last leak in the sky. As she was repairing it, a grain of sand fell from the sky down to the earth, and hit the ground into a lake, which is now Xuanwu Lake; the rest part of the sand standing at the lake as a mountain, which is now Purple Mountain.

The myth of "Nüwa mending the sky" is well-known in China, and has taken root in traditional Chinese culture. Nüwa devoted her life to protecting human beings, for what she had wished to create was a world where human beings could live in peace, and her pursuit of and devotion to peace were passed down from generation to generation.

Nanjing, the Ancient Capital

A Land of Beauty and Goodness

Mr. Sun Yat-sen once praised Nanjing as a "land of beauty and goodness" in his *Guidelines for the Founding of a Country*: "This land has three kinds of heavenly craftsmanship, high mountains, deep waters, and open plains. It is hard to find such a perfect place among the other metropolises in the world." Thus, Nanjing was chosen to be capital by the National Government of the Republic of China in 1927. It once again became the political, military and cultural center of the country. Its inclusiveness and enterprise cultivated by the historical accumulation over centuries has also destined that Nanjing must be at the forefront of the times and lead China on the journey to modernization.

After the capital was established here, the Nanjing National Government decided to make an overall plan for its development. At the beginning of 1929, the government organized the Capital Construction Committee, appointing Sun Ke, son of Sun Yat-sen, as the person in charge. The famous American architectural engineer Henry Killam Murphy, who had designed Tsinghua Academy, together with his assistant Ernest P. Goodrich, was specially invited to compile *The City Plan of Nanking* and it was officially launched on December 31, 1929. This was the first complete urban plan in the history of Nanjing and set the pace for its modernization.

Murphy was appointed chief architectural consultant for the national government on the city planning. He had unique insights in many fields such as planning methods, urban design, and project management. He was committed to maintaining the traditional features of Chinese architecture, attempting to achieve a combination of Chinese and Western styles in order to create a "true Chinese" metropolis while using the advanced planning methods of Europe and America. His goal was to use "Chinese traditional architectural style to design all new buildings" and "to avoid destroying China's beautiful heritage by following Western styles".

The City Plan of Nanking was rich in content, including the reckoned population of Nanjing in a next century, which determined the geographical boundaries of the capital, the central political district, the administrative district, the building forms, waterways and railways, parks, schools, housing and industrial areas, and even the airport, all conceived and arranged in the scheme. The plan combined Chinese and Western cultures and all were designed for a next century, aiming to build Nanjing into an Eastern "Washington DC", and selecting Purple Mountain as the "Capitol Hill" of China. The dream about a modern city was described on paper, and it was from here that the grand plan and goal to "strive for the equality and freedom in China", "arouse the people and unite the other nations worldwide that treat my nation equally to fight together" were set in motion.

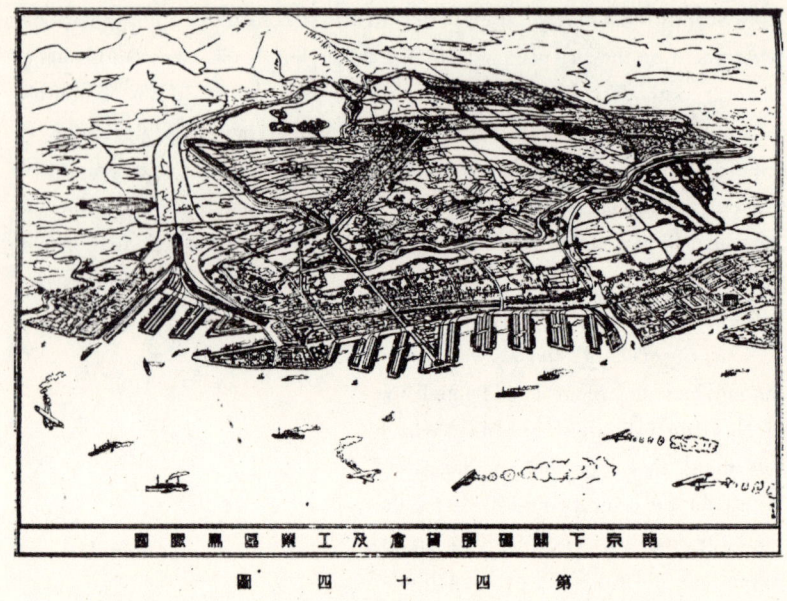

Fig.1-3 Aerial View of the Warehouse and Industrial Area of Nanjing Xiaguan Dock in Scheme 44 of *The City Plan of Nanjing*

Genius Poet Li Bai and "Jinling"

Many people say that "Jinling" is the most beautiful name for the ancient capital, Nanjing. Li Bai, a great poet in the Tang Dynasty, had a strong feeling for Nanjing. Although he wandered across the country, he stayed in Jinling for the longest time. He loved the beautiful things of Jinling so much that he wrote more than 100 poems about the city, and among them was that "The topography is fit for the emperor's residence, the mountains like a coiling dragon and a crouching tiger. The Jinling Mountain is barely magnificent in appearance, and the natural barrier isn't safe as once". He also repeatedly used Jinling to implicitly express his feeling of nostalgia in his "Mounting Jinling Phoenix Terrace", "The terrace once phoenixes roaming, sees no phoenix but the Yangtze River flowing. The path in the Wu palace is overgrown with weeds, the cenotaph of the Jin Dynasty reduced to barrows of Jinling. Beyond the azure sky Triple Mountain rising, aside winds the river Egret Islet's half cutting. As the clouds are always covering the sun, Chang'an afar keeps me worrying!" His poetic feelings passed down on have enriched people's love for Jinling.

Prosperous Metropolis

After the capital of the national government established in Nanjing, it quickly evolved into the business and financial center of the country. The prosperous market economy provided a guarantee for the civilians' harmonious and happy life. At that time, there were three main business districts in Nanjing, one was the Confucius Temple business district in the south of the city; the second was the famous commercial street—Xinjiekou; the third was the Xiaguan commercial district on the bank of the Yangtze River in the north of the city.

Fig.1-4 Nanjing Xinjiekou Commercial District during the Republic of China

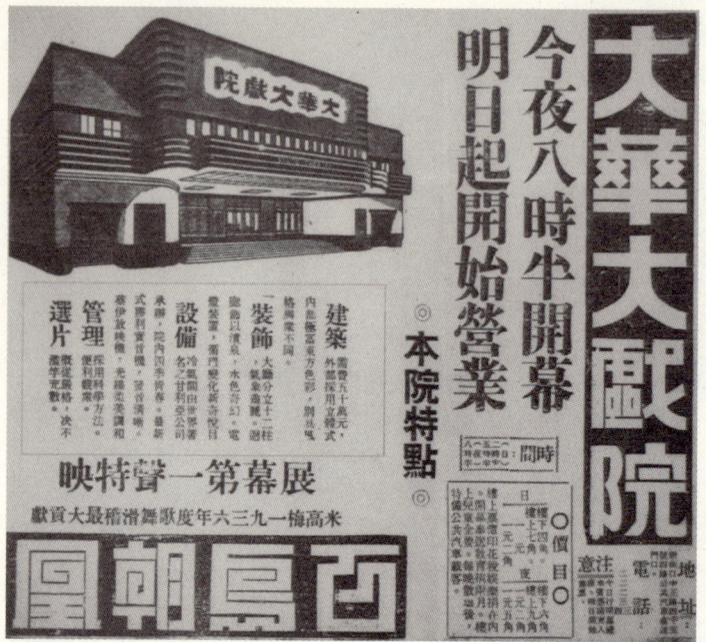

Fig.1-5 News about the Opening of Dahua Theatre (1936)

The commercial center enriched the citizens' cultural and entertainment life, and seeing films was the fashionable choice of casual dating. There were so-called "Four Famous Theaters in the capital of Republic of China", the Capital Grand Theater, Dahua Theater, World Theater, Xindu Theater. The Capital Grand Theater was the first theater in China to be equipped with a central air-conditioning system. It was one of the earliest theaters in China to show films indoors instead of outdoors, and it had more than 1,000 seats on the upper and lower floors. The scale and facilities of Dahua Theater were ranked at the top in the country. Its premiere film was the musical *Birds Pay Homage* produced by MGM Corporation, which was the first foreign film that many people were exposed to there. Dahua Theater also received many Chinese art groups and famous artists. For example, Mr. Mei Lanfang, master of Peking Opera, once gave a benefit performance there to raise money for the flooded area. Nanjing residents rushed to buy tickets, and soon raised a lot of donations, which became a good story.

The Xiaguan area was the junction of the Tianjin-Pukou Line, the Shanghai-Nanjing Line and the Yangtze River Channel, and it was also an important transportation hub of Nanjing to the external area. In October 1933, the Nanjing Railway Ferry, the first railway ferry in Asia, began to run. For a time, there was a lot of traffic and people, and it became the only place for passengers and goods to pass through. Shops were lined up around the ferry, such as pig shops, cattle shops, chicken shops, rice

Fig.1-6 Xiaguan Dock in the 1930s

shops, and so on, attracting customers across the country, and thus this area was called "Big Road". Its prosperity was once comparable to the Confucius Temple business area, so it was also known as "the Confucius Temple in the south and the Big Road in the north". In 1934, the Ministry of Railways opened a through train from Shanghai to Peiping (Beijing). The journey took 34 hours. With the "Yangtze River" Train Ferry, passengers could travel from Shanghai to Beijing without changing trains. Taking the train became a fashionable move at that time, and many wealthy newlyweds chose to take this train for their honeymoon trip.

When Liu Jiwen, the first mayor of Nanjing took office, he began to build Zhongshan Road [Fig.1-7]. This road, about 12 kilometers long, was originally built to transport Mr. Sun Yat-sen's coffin when it was moved from Beijing to Nanjing via the Xiaguan Dock. The dock was then renamed Zhongshan Dock, so was the asphalt road Zhongshan Avenue as an eternal memorial. As the first asphalt road in Nanjing, the wide and straight Zhongshan Avenue was the landmark of the capital. The road was lined with trees and buildings in unique styles, leading to the downtown area. Subsequently, in accordance with *The City Plan of Nanking*, nearly a hundred roads including Taiping Road, and Baixia Road were successively built. After ten years of construction, Nanjing had completed more than 120 kilometers of roads by the beginning of 1937, laying the foundation for modern Nanjing.

Fig.1-7 Zhongshan Road under Construction

Fig.1-8 Zhongshan Dock Today

Transportation in nature is a form of "linking", bridging gaps between people, regions and countries. In 1933, the Nanjing National Government rebuilt the Zhongshan Dock, and built Jiangnan Railway and a ring road linking Nanjing Station of the Jiangnan Railway with the Shanghai-Nanjing Railway. The Dajiaochang Airport, built in 1929 and covering a total land area of about 10 square kilometers, was one of the largest aviation bases in China's history and one of the airports with the best facilities at that time. The next year, the National Government set up a joint venture with the United States and Germany to establish China Airlines and Eurasian Airlines, opening air routes from Nanjing to major cities across the country and all over the world.

Peace is not isolated from other things. The development of economy and transportation calls for a peaceful environment. With peace, economy can develop in an orderly manner and people can live and work in contentment. With the well-developed transportation, people can have an open mind, and connect with each other and the world. This also allows us to understand why this city has such an ardent expectation for peace when facing difficulties and distress; it also makes us sigh for the prosperity that would be broken by war.

Garden City

The urban park is the main public open space in a city and it is an explicit symbol of the modernization of the human settlement environment. After the capital of the National Government established in Nanjing, the construction of the urban landscape was also put on the agenda. *The City Plan of Nanking* specially devoted a chapter to "Parks and Boulevards" to emphasize the importance of urban landscape, pointing out that "the setting of parks is vital to the health and happiness of citizens", and planning to build more than ten scenic spots throughout Nanjing to make it a garden city with Eastern style. In addition to the existing parks like Zhongshan Cemetery, Xuanwu Lake Park, First Park, Gulou Park, and Qinhuai Park, parks were also arranged in Yuhuatai, Mochou Lake, Qingliang Mountain, Xinjiekou, Chaotian Palace, Xiaguan and other places. The National Government also added varieties of flowers and trees to the existing scenic spots, repaired pavilions, and set up children's playgrounds and memorial buildings, etc., in order to better play the entertainment and education functions of the park.

Fig.1-9 Xuanwu Lake Park in the 1930s

At the opening ceremony of Xuanwu Lake Park in 1928, Liu Jiwen, the mayor of Nanjing, said that the lake would be made into the most beautiful amusement park, where visitors could read books and newspapers, go fishing, play basketball and enjoy other entertainment. In 1936, there were seven completed parks, and eight were under construction or planned to build in Nanjing.

The boulevards between the parks were also included in the government's plan. Besides Zhongshan Avenue, 25 boulevards were included in the plan, like Changjiang Road, Huangpu Road, and Zhongyang Road. Scale standards that were most suitable for the landscape were stipulated by the designers, in the hope of turning Nanjing into a huge urban park. Purple Mountain, which was overgrown with weeds, became lush and green after the restoration work. After more than ten years of hard work, the occupancy of parks and boulevards inside and outside Nanjing reached 14%. Its green area proportion was no less than that of international metropolises such as Washington DC, Paris, London and Tokyo at that time, and was at the world's leading level.

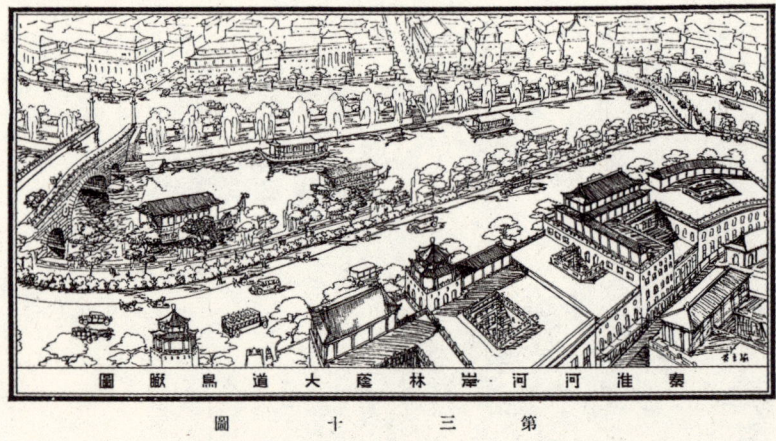

Fig.1-10 Aerial View of the Boulevards on the Banks of the Qinhuai River in Scheme 30 of *The City Plan of Nanking*

Residents' Unique Love for Plane Trees

The plane tree is an iconic logo of Nanjing. In the writing of Ye Zhaoyan, "people's first impression of Nanjing was this first-class greening, and the prominent symbol of this greening was the plane trees planted on both sides of Zhongshan Avenue and on the green roundabouts in the middle of the streets. No one knew how many plane trees there were in Nanjing... This was an opulent surrounding that had never been seen in any other city in China." In 1929, Nanjing planted tens of thousands of plane trees for Mr. Sun Yat-sen and they seemed like the guards standing at his bier. These trees were carefully pruned into a posture of three upward branches, each 6 meters tall and 6 trees in a row, like "tall guards" protecting the city. In the eyes of the old inhabitants, they are not just trees, but image of the omnipresent green streetscape long kept in their mind. However, they were cut down in large numbers in the 1990s for dredging the road traffic construction. This felling operation caused many residents to protest and it had to be suspended. Now, the plane trees are still flourishing and vigorous, and this unique love for plane trees continues in the hearts of the young generation.

Fig.1-11 **Plane Trees**

Tangible Memory of Peace

The city is like a palace of memories. Almost every street and building has witnessed the history, displayed the history and constructed a period of historical memory. Zhu Ziqing, a famous writer, once wrote, "Walking in Nanjing is like visiting an antique shop. The traces of erosion left by time can be found everywhere. It is the tangible memory of this city that you can touch, pay tribute to, and contemplate leisurely..." The architecture has seen the transformation of Nanjing over centuries and left a unique mark of peace on the city.

Nanjing City Wall of the Ming Dynasty

Nanjing City Wall of the Ming Dynasty is like the patron saint of the city. Though built for the sake of war, it was born to protect peace. It represented the boundary of the city, and also symbolized the stability of it. It has stood here for hundreds of years, witnessing the change of times. With a silent and firm body, it guards this prosperous city and brings peace to its inhabitants.

Fig.1-12 Nanjing City Wall in the 1920s

Nanjing City Wall of the Ming Dynasty, extensively built in the early Ming Dynasty, has a history of more than 600 years. It included the four-layered walls of the Palace City, Imperial City, Capital City and Outer City, which were built in the Ming Dynasty. It is now preserved intact for 25.1 kilometers. As the largest ancient city wall in China, it is a common cultural heritage of mankind. The city wall was unique in its construction and layout, boldly abandoning the traditional square and formal image of an ancient capital city, making full use of the inherent topography of Nanjing and was built on the hillsides and the river banks, quite strong, easy to defend and difficult to attack. It was considered to be a masterpiece of artistic and military design at the time. There were 13 gates of the inner city wall during the Ming Dynasty.

Zhonghua Gate was the most complex castle-like city gate among them, and was known as "the first urn city in the world" [Fig.1-13]. Inside the city gate were three urn cities, four arches, and 27 standing-rooms in the middle of the wall. In actual combat, a large flashboard, after the enemy entered the first city wall gate, would be dropped for the soldiers in the standing-rooms to ambush the enemy in the strategy of "catching turtles in the urn". Before and behind the Zhonghua Gate, the Qinhuai River, traversing east and west, connected this prosperous area to the south of the Yangtze River.

Zhu Yuanzhang, founding emperor of the Ming Dynasty, was particularly concerned about this magnificent project. The construction of the city wall was under his direct supervision. According to his requirement, the side of each brick was printed with the names of the producers. Moreover, special quality controllers were ordered to test the brick quality by colliding them. If bricks were not broken, they were considered qualified. If they hit and broke, not only substitutions would be produced, but the related personnel would also be

Fig.1-13 The First Urn City in the World—Zhonghua Gate

Fig.1-14 Nanjing City Wall of the Ming Dynasty Today

punished; if they failed to pass for a second time, the brick-burner may face the risk of decapitation. The number of characters engraved on the surface of the bricks was up to 69, and it preserved a lot of precious information about history, science and technology, and humanities. These characters, in the form of regular script, running script, cursive script, seal script, and official script, can be clearly seen to this day. One can still feel the warmth of history when wandering on and touching those weather-beaten grey bricks.

The city wall is a landmark of this city. It defends the boundaries of the city and maintains the social stability of it. The construction of the city wall reflects a form of defense, which demonstrates the ancient people's wish for stability and their understanding of peace. In fact, as early as the

Spring and Autumn Period and the Warring States Period, Mo Zi, the famous Chinese thinker, put forward the thought of universal love and defensive war. During his time, there were continuous wars in various places, and the people had no way to live out. Mo Zi believed that if one could love others and treated others' bodies as one's own body, no wars would be launched. Therefore, he advocated that everyone in the world should love each other regardless of lowliness and nobleness. But he also realized that it was not enough to just call for the cessation of wars and to love each other. Measures must be taken to stop wars; that is to say, the idea of defense must be emphasized. His thought was also absorbed by military strategists of the following dynasties. Hence, the ancient city wall, just stands in the passing of time, guarding the joy and peace of the city's residents.

Ascending the City Wall in Hope of Peace

Nanjing residents have the habit of going up to the city wall on the 16th of the first lunar month. It is said that walking on the top of the city wall that day can "eliminate all diseases" and "drive away mishaps".

This custom originated from the late Ming and early Qing Dynasties. In the old days, men and women, old and young, all climbed up the city wall, in the hope of "eliminating all diseases" for the old, and "gaining promotion step by step" for the young. Now this is still part of the popular customs of Nanjing residents. At the beginning of the year when the weather turns warmer, the whole family goes out and walks on the top of the city wall to enjoy the city landscape, and at the same time express their simple wish for the social harmony and peace.

Fig.1-15 Climbing the City Wall

Divine Creature Bixie

Bixie was a kind of divine creature in ancient China. Like the Nanjing City Wall, it is also the vivid symbol of the long history of Nanjing, guarding the city's peace. The original meaning of bixie referred to "deviant evil rather than righteousness", and has been extended to ward off evils and turn evil into good fortune. On this base, the ancient people created this ancient creature like a lion with wings. This beast looks majestic in appearance, and solemn and dignified, which highly combines the sense of strength and art.

In Nanjing, Bixie can often be seen decorated in images, pattern designs or replicas of bronze or stone carvings. The stone sculpture of Bixie [Fig.1-16] was carved from a whole block of boulder, some of which weighed more than 15 tons. Bixie also implies that Nanjing was the ancient capital of China, and the residence of the emperor, and had the mountains that looked like a coiling dragon or a crouching tiger, so it once appeared on the city emblem of Nanjing. This creature is also a symbol of peace in Nanjing today, endowed with various connotations of peace, like resisting violence, promoting prosperity, and eliminating disease.

Fig.1-16 A Stone Sculpture of Bixie in Nanjing

Fraternity of Sun Yat-sen

In the spring of 1912, Sun Yat-sen, together with his colleagues and friends, hunted in the Zhongshan Mountain. When the group sat down to take a rest, Sun Yat-sen was attracted by the beautiful mountain, majestic and winding, looking like a giant dragon wandering from a distance. It was lush and green, the purple air was rising, and nature and humanities coexisted. He could not restrain uttering a sigh, "When I died, I'd like to beg the nation for a handful of this soil for a last resting place." In 1925, Sun Yat-sen died of illness in Beijing, and according to his will, his remains was transported back to Nanjing, where he would sleep forever. In May 1925, Sun Yat-sen's Funeral Preparation Office invited tenders for the architectural designs for the mausoleum from home and abroad. The invitation for bid caused a sensation in the architecture and art circles, and many people applied for it. Lü Yanzhi, a 31-year architect, stood out from more than 40 bidders and won the first prize. In order to design the Sun Yat-sen Mausoleum well, he kept optimizing the design plan all day long with no appetite for food and drinks. For the sake of direct vision, every time he drew a draft, he used tung oil putty to pinch out the model, and then repeatedly modify it. The hard work paid off, and his design [Fig.1-17] finally stood out and won the favor of Song Qingling, Mr. Sun's wife. After the design draft was finalized, Lü Yanzhi, as he wished, invited Yao Xizhou to build the main structure of Sun Yat-sen Mausoleum. The slope of Purple Mountain was quite steep, and it was almost impossible to move hundreds of tons of granite up to the site. Under the circumstances that both the geographical environment and the budget were very challenging, Yao Xizhou, despite sleeping and eating in the open air, led his building team

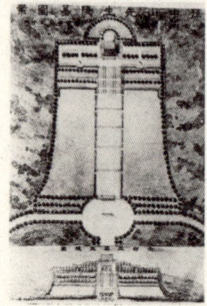

Fig.1-17 The Blueprint of Sun Yat-sen Mausoleum by Lü Yanzhi

Fig.1-18 Sun Yat-sen Mausoleum around 1930

to complete the construction of this huge project as scheduled, because they admired for Sun Yat-sen, a great man of the time, even if it was unprofitable.

Sun Yat-sen Mausoleum was finally completed in 1929, covering an area of approximately 80,000 square meters (about 20 acres). The cemetery was built with Purple Mountain at the back, and its layout generally presented an erected "gigantic bell", implying that Mr. Sun Yat-sen had devoted his life to "arousing the people" and it was known as "the first tomb in the history of modern Chinese architecture".

Fig.1-19 Sun Yat-sen Mausoleum Today

    The design of Sun Yat-sen Mausoleum is an architecture model in modern Chinese architecture, blending the modern style with the national style. The overall plan absorbed the characteristics of ancient Chinese royal tombs, adopting an axis-symmetrical arrangement. The mausoleum was built on the slope of the mountain, and used the components of a traditional tomb such as archway, passageway, gate, stele pavilion, mourning hall, vault, and specifically referred to the design of some famous European tombs, such as the mourning hall of the Lincoln Memorial. It was like a "hybrid" building, absorbing elements from the history of the East and the West, and carrying forward the concept of "merging the East and the West" advocated by Mr. Sun Yat-sen during his lifetime. "Open monumentality" is another feature of Sun Yat-sen Mausoleum, which is not only simple and solemn, but also close to the people, and at the same time possesses the immortal value of Chinese culture and art, expressing the remembrance of the great man and his immortal spirit.

Fig.1-20 Stone Archway of Sun Yat-sen Mausoleum

    The two Chinese characters "bo ai" (fraternity) in Sun Yat-sen's handwriting were engraved in the center of the stone archway of Sun Yat-sen Mausoleum [Fig.1-20], which was the finishing touch of the entire architecture complex. Sun Yat-sen cared about the people's livelihood all his life and took the freedom of the masses as his own duty. "Bo ai" was the quintessence of his thought and his highest ideal. As for the meaning of "bo ai", he once said, "Because our pursuit of people's livelihood is to make four hundred million people happy, and to seek happiness for them is what 'bo ai' refers to." Sun mentioned in his will, "we must arouse the people and unite the other nations worldwide that treat my nation equally to fight together" to achieve permanent peace in the world. These two Chinese characters were sculptured by the architect Lü Yanzhi on the transom above the archway that led to the mausoleum, which highlighted Mr. Sun's love of the nation, of the country, mankind, and peace. He sowed the seeds of universal love in the hearts of the people of Nanjing, and the spiritual connotation of this building complex will last for generations.

Origin of Jinling Culture

The Qinhuai River is the "mother river" of Nanjing. It is an eternal topic in the hearts of Nanjing people, because it is the origin of the ancient city of Jinling and the cradle of Nanjing culture. According to legend, when Emperor Qin Shihuang visited eastward to Jinling, he was informed by an alchemist that Jinling was a city with an auspicious sign from an emperor. Rather than risk losing his territory, Emperor Qin Shihuang had a river dug to break the dragon veins of the city, which was called the "Qinhuai" River.

The Qinhuai River includes the inner river and the external river. The "ten-li Qinhuai" in history refers to the inner river, which is the essence of the Qinhuai scenery zone. On the south river bank there is a large screen wall with two dragons playing bead on it, and it was built in the third year of Wanli in the Ming Dynasty (1575), with a total length of 110 meters and a height of 10 meters [Fig.1-21]. High and majestic, it is now the largest preserved screen wall in the country. Along the riverbanks, there are sculptures of Eight Beauties of Qinhuai, Dongshuiguan (water-controlling facilities in the east of the city) Heritage Park, Qinhuai Shui Pavilion (pavilions on the riverbank), Taoye Ferry, Bailuzhou Park (Egrets Park), Jiangnan Gongyuan (Jiangnan Examination Hall), WangDao XieAn Memorial Hall, Li Xiangjun's Former Residence, Zhanyuan (History Museum of Taiping Heavenly Kingdom), Qin Dashi's Former Residence, and Shen Wansan Former Residence. The river also connects tourist and cultural attractions such as Urn City of Zhonghua Gate.

Fig.1-21 Two Dragons Playing Bead on the Screen Wall

The Qinhuai River, the famous river in the Chinese historical culture, has a reputation of "Cultural Hub under Heaven", with diversified cultures gathering here. There has never been such a river that is so closely tied to the destiny of Chinese intellectuals. During the Eastern Jin Dynasty, the "Imperial College" was established on the banks of the Qinhuai River. In the Northern Song Dynasty, a temple was expanded here to worship scholar-official Confucius, which was known as "the Confucian Temple". In the fourth year of Qiandao in the Southern Song Dynasty (1168), Jiangnan Examination Hall was completed here. After its repair and expansion through ages, it reached its peak during the Ming and Qing Dynasties. During

Fig.1-22 Mingyuan Building of Jiangnan Examination Hall during the Republic of China

the Tongzhi period of the Qing Dynasty, it could accommodate more than 20,000 candidates for examinations at a time. Until the abolition of the imperial examination system in the late Qing Dynasty, more than 800 champions were chosen from here for the country. During the Ming and Qing Dynasties alone, more than half of the officials came from the Jiangnan Examination Hall, which fulfilled its sacred mission of "selecting talents for the country". No matter where they were born, and no matter where they came from, once they walked into the Jiangnan Examination Hall, the candidates would feel that they were already shouldering the responsibility for the masses and for the country. Their ten-year study at the cold window attracted little attention, only when their names were in the list of the successes. They would devote their wisdom and virtue and do their best to serve the country afterwards.

It is unlikely to know exactly how many scholars once roaming on the banks of the Qinhuai River, and how many poems were created and spread for ages. For example, "Mist veiling the cold water while moonlight shining on the banks, by night we moored on the Qinhuai River near some pubs. The actress worried little about a subjugated country, across the river singing the 'Rear-Court Flowers'", from *Mooring on the Qinhuai River* by Du Mu, a poet of the Tang Dynasty; and "Swallows nestling under Wang's and Xie's roofs in the past, flew into the houses of ordinary people", the widely spread sentence from *Wuyi Lane* poem by Liu Yuxi. The beauty of Qinhuai River was depicted in the lines of the poets, while the fates of the family and the country filled the poets' heart. "If you hold a high office in the royal court, you should take the responsibility for the life of the masses; if you are a civilian staying far away from the royal court, you should also concern about the state affairs." It was in such words that Chinese intellectuals, literati and officials expounded their ideals of making the country prosperous, and their worries about the chaotic conditions under heaven. Among them were such historical celebrities as Chen Duxiu, Lin

Fig.1-23 Rooms of the Jiangnan Examination Hall during the Republic of China

Fig.1-24 The Qinhuai River in the 1920s

Zexu, Wei Yuan, Li Hongzhang, Zhang Zhidong, and so on, who influenced Nanjing and China at different times in the history. The wheel of history keeps moving forward. The landscapes, like the Golden Phoenix Tower on the river, gaily-painted boats rowing on the gentle waves, and the gurgle and lamplights, are still fascinated. The memory of the Jinling history originated from the Qinhuai River, and its moving legends continue to be written in the changing memories.

Fig.1-25 The Qinhuai River Today

The Urban Character

Speaking of Nanjing in the Republic of China, Nie Gannu, a poet, once commented, "When I first arrived at Nanjing, there was not a wide and flat road in the city. The streets were full of dilapidated and low tile houses... After one year or two years, five years or ten years, it completely changed with the best asphalt roads in the country, magnificent halls, government offices, schools, theaters, businesses shops, restaurants, coffee shops and even private residences..." Let's take a walk on the streets and alleys to enjoy the hustle and

Fig.1-26 Streets of Nanjing in the 1930s

bustle of the urban life, for they preserve the individual memory of the city, appreciate its feelings and character, and perceive its simplicity and tolerance in the eye of a native of Nanjing.

Food and People's Character Traits

Food is the most direct and important way of reflecting the culture of a city. All kinds of delicacies epitomize the daily life of the Nanjing residents, and their preference for food reveals their character traits from another angle.

Teahouses [Fig.1-27] were one of the most popular places frequented by the dwellers in Nanjing. All over the streets and alleys were various kinds of teahouses, a tea stand with a few tables and benches, or a teahouse with fine decorations. There were 20 to 30 teahouses in the business area of Confucius Temple alone, forming a unique tea culture. The names of the teahouses were varied, most of which have the Chinese characters with auspicious meanings, such as *fu*, *shun*, *xing*, *tai*, *an*, etc. But no matter what conditions the teahouse was in, it mattered little for guests to go there for pastime. Whenever you went there, you'd find the teahouse was packed with tea drinkers. With a pot of tea and a few plates of side dishes, one could enjoy the leisure time of a whole day. Frequenting the teahouse was not only to enjoy tea and talk, or to relax and have fun, but also to discuss official affairs or exchange information for many dignitaries and businessmen. Moreover, it was also a stage for many folk artists to make a living, where they played musical instruments and sang folk songs for the guests. Today Nanjing Laomendong cultural and historical streets replicate the original appearance of the streets and alleys in the south of the old city, where there were white walls and black tiles, wooden corridor gardens, and many teahouses. A wooden teahouse built according to the old-style teahouse [Fig.1-28] is also on display in the Nanjing Museum's exhibition hall of the Republic of China. There you can experience the unique charm of Nanjing tea culture.

Fig.1-27 Old Nanjing Teahouse

Fig.1-28 Old-Style Teahouse in Nanjing Museum

The vegetable market was also an indispensable memory in ordinary civilians' daily life. In his novel *Danfeng Street*, Zhang Henshui, a famous writer, detailed the characteristics of the vegetable market in Danfeng Street in Nanjing, "Twenty or thirty open-air stalls piled up old green or tender green vegetables. In front of them were fresh fish stalls… The men and women carrying baskets shouldered their way… This street, half a *li* long, was packed with people and baskets from dawn till ten o'clock in the morning. Rice shops, charcoal shops, sauce shops, and grocery stores were all in this street, grabbing business in this busiest time." The hustle and bustle, the noise of people, was pictured as lively scenes of the residents' ordinary life.

What must be mentioned is the inhabitants' favor for eating duck. They have the tradition of eating duck since the Qing Dynasty. Duck may be prepared in many ways, such as "salted duck", "duck salted with osmanthus flowers", "pressed salted duck", "roast duck", "duck's four parts" and "duck blood with starch vermicelli", all of which are delicacy on the table of the residents. Salted duck can be made all year round, and it can be consumed by both senior officials and ordinary civilians because of its fair price. The cooked duck in whole has a distended body, fresh luster, fragrant and tender meat. The fat mixed with the sweetness of duck meat fills the mouth, fat but not greasy, stimulating your appetite, quite unforgettable. When free, invite some friends or relatives to take some duck, gnaw its four parts, and have a drink, happy like a fairy! Even the paltry duck oil is used to its extreme, and pancakes cooked with it have become a specialty snack. Many residents start their day with a mouthful of duck-oil pancakes [Fig.1-29], a bite of the freshly-baked duck-oil pancakes, crispy and fragrant, with a long aftertaste. The memories on the tongue are a kind of nostalgia, as well as continuity of the happy life.

Fig.1-29 Duck-Oil Pancakes

"Nanjing Turnips"

Foreigners who first came to Nanjing may have heard of "Nanjing turnips". Turnip is a common vegetable, rich in nutrients and easy to grow. Although it is not a specialty of Nanjing, it is favored by the inhabitants in the extreme, and made into a variety of turnip meals, sweet and sour turnip, turnip salad, braised turnip, fried turnip, stewed turnip, and so on. The turnip is a good match, and it can go easy with other cooking materials such as pork, beef, sheep, seafood, that kind of thing to create authentic delicacies. The turnip is also incarnate in the image of Nanjing people, which is a metaphor for their character traits of inclusiveness, simplicity and forthrightness.

Architectural Styles

Architecture is a solidified memory. It has witnessed the growth of the city and added luster to its beauty. As the capital of the Republic of China, Nanjing was second to none in the country in terms of the architectural quantity, style, material and function. The buildings of the Republic of China are unique in blending Chinese and Western styles, and they are also a microcosm of its urban culture. These buildings also undertake social functions in the fields of science, education, culture, and health, and play an irreplaceable social value. As a result, the image of the former capital is consolidated and exaggerated, and spread and imagined as the time goes by.

The City Plan of Nanking divided the residential buildings into four levels. Villas and garden houses were at the first level; apartments and ordinary buildings were at the second and third levels; at the fourth level were shanty towns. The National Government specially named the roads of the newly planned residential areas with "Chinese Famous Scenic Spots". For example, the main road was called "Yihe", while the branch roads were "Luojia", "Lingyin", "Putuo", "Chibi", "Mogan", "Guling", and "Langya", which were quite rich in Chinese classical culture. The 287 detached buildings in the garden community, built successively in 1933, were mostly two-storied Western-style houses, collectively reflecting the high-end residences of Nanjing during the Republic of China. Thus, it is said that a community of Yihe Road carries half of the history of the Republic of China. This garden community almost becomes a "small exhibition hall" of Western-styled architecture.

Fig.1-30 Residential Area of Yihe Road Today

In the memory of Nanjing civilians, Yihe Road community was the residential area for the upper class and foreigners. Senior politicians of the National Government and foreign envoys, such as Chen Cheng, Chen Bulei, Yu Youren, Yan Xishan, Tang Enbo, and Marshall, the special envoy of the US president, all once lived in this newly-built community. Thus, many thrilling stories going around these important figures started from here, and they witnessed the vital moments one after another that asserted influence on Nanjing, which inherited the history and highlighted the future. When you walk on Yihe Road, the buildings in front of you are the physical symbols of the history of Nanjing over a century, witnessing the change of times, miniaturizing the previous prosperity and preserving the taste of Nanjing in the Republic of China.

There is a villa in Nanjing University, which was also a famous building in the Republic of China. This villa was the former residence of Pearl S. Buck [Fig.1-31], an American writer, spending her childhood, adolescence and youth in China, and China could be counted as her second hometown. Her husband served as a professor at the Agricultural College of Jinling University. The couple spent 8 years in this villa. In 1921 Pearl S. Buck came to Jinling University, the predecessor of Nanjing University, to work as a teacher at the Department of Foreign Languages, and she also taught pedagogy, English and other courses in the National Central University, another predecessor of Nanjing University. She lived and studied for many years in China, which gave her great creative inspiration so that her novel *The Good Earth* won the Nobel Prize in Literature in 1938. This book tries to reveal the life process of Chinese farmers, their birth, ageing, sickness, death, joys and sorrows, and it is hailed as an "epic description of the life of the Chinese farmers". What is touching is the unyielding force in this simple soul, and it also shows the world, especially the West, the Chinese people's courage to pursue a better life. She was once praised as "a bridge between Eastern and Western civilizations" by former US President Nixon.

People Who Love Freedom

On December 10, 1938, Pearl S. Buck, the Nobel Prize winner in literature that year, ended her brief acceptance speech with the following assertion at the award ceremony held in Stockholm: "I should not be truly myself if I did not, in my own wholly unofficial way, speak also of the people of China, whose life has for so many years been my life also, whose life, indeed, must always be a part of my life. The minds of my own country and of China, my foster country, are alike in many ways, but above all, alike in our common love of freedom. And today more than ever, this is true, now when China's whole being is engaged in the greatest of all struggles, the struggles for freedom. I have never admired China more than I do now, when I see her uniting as she has never before, against the enemy who threatens her freedom. With this determination for freedom, which is in so profound a sense the essential quality in her nature, I know that she is unconquerable."

Fig.1-31 Former Residence of Pearl S. Buck

Education, Culture and Sports

The character of a city is inseparable from its education, culture and sports. During the Republic of China, Nanjing's science, education, culture and sports were always in a leading position in the country. Groups of Chinese education pioneers and reformers came to this city with dreams to find an education model suitable for Chinese youth. Their exploration and contribution to education guided the development of Nanjing and even China.

In the spring of 1923, the first experimental kindergarten for preschool education in modern Chinese history was established in Nanjing, named "Nanjing Private Gulou Kindergarten". The founder was Chen Heqin, a professor of child psychology in the Department of Education of Southeast University. In 1936, the number of primary schools in Nanjing increased to 231, with nearly 80,000 pupils and more than 2,000 faculty members, and 80% of school-aged children had enrolled in school.

Nanjing was also one of the earliest cities to carry out teacher education. In March 1927, Tao Xingzhi founded the Xiaozhuang Experimental Rural Normal School in Nanjing, which was later renamed Xiaozhuang School. In this school, educational concepts, such as "life is education", "society is school" and "unity of teaching and learning", were

Fig.1-32 Old Photo of Xiaozhuang School

established. Tao Xingzhi believed that life itself was a kind of vivid education, so it was necessary to liberate children's minds and hands, encourage them to contact with the society, and enable them to fully enjoy a free life. His belief, "only when education is for the public can a fair world come into being", reflected the highest realm of education. It meant that education was supposed to put aside selfishness, teach without discrimination, and finally achieve an ideal society, and the world would become one.

Fig.1-33 Auditorium at the Former Site of Central University

Higher education in Nanjing was relatively advanced and became a model in the country. By the beginning of 1937, there'd been 8 colleges and universities in Nanjing, including the Private Jinling University and the Private Jinling Women's College of Arts and Sciences, ranking first in the country.

National Central University was the largest university with the most comprehensive faculties and departments, and it was also the predecessor of today's Nanjing University, Southeast University Nanjing Normal University and many other universities. Here elites and masters gathered, such as the geologist Li Siguang, the physicist Wu Youxun, the biologist Tong Dizhou, the meteorologist Zhu Kezhen, the bridge expert Mao Yisheng, the poet Xu Zhimo, the educator Tao Xingzhi, and so on. They reflected the spirit and character of this city, and spread scientific knowledge to forge new generations for the development of the country.

The Private Jinling University was a famous university at that time. It was merged from the four academies founded by the American Church, and came into being in 1910. It was renamed Jinling University in August 1951 after being combined with Jinling Women's College of Arts and Sciences. Due to the influence of the American Church, Jinling University adopted American education approach and was strict with students. According to Mr. Zhang Kaiyuan, the rejection rate of Jinling University was very high, "There were many assignments and many reference books for students; the seats were arranged in the alphabet sequence of the first letter of names in English during class. The teacher would stand on the stage and look around the class, which was clear at a glance that who had arrived and who had not"; "Then what were the consequences for students who didn't want to study and just played? As you know, they couldn't graduate". In the history department where he studied, only one quarter of the enrolled students could get a bachelor's degree. Jinling University paid special attention to fostering students' virtue and their spirit of benevolence. Therefore, the relationships between teachers and students and within students were very harmonious, which made people feel warm, tolerant and kind in their study and life. The spirit of benevolence and mutual help benefited many people throughout their lives. Jinling University set a good example for the establishment and development of modern university education in China. The outstanding talents from here were distributed in China and abroad, and they made achievements in various fields and were well-known in the world.

Fig.1-34 Panorama of Jinling University during the Republic of China

Fig.1-35 Building 100, Jinling Women's University during the Republic of China

Jinling Women's College, China's first women's university, was also in Nanjing. It was founded in 1915 by the alliance of seven churches including the American Christian Church, the Presbyterian Church, and the London Church in England, and was one of the famous missionary universities during the Republic of China and enjoyed a reputation in the country. The motto of this college was to "improve people's living condition", which Wu Yifang, the principal, explained that this was to tell the students that "the purpose of one's life is not only for themselves, but also to help others with their own wisdom and ability to enrich their lives".

Fig.1-36 Building 100, Suiyuan Campus, Nanjing Normal University

In 1922, the college selected its site on Ninghai Road. The early construction of the college was jointly completed by Lü Yanzhi, the famous architect and chief designer of Sun Yat-sen Mausoleum, together with Murphy, his American teacher. Murphy adopted the axis and courtyard layout of the Forbidden City for reference in his design, and used Western concrete structure to build the pillars and bucket arches in imitation of Chinese architecture. In this way, Murphy expressed his love for Chinese classical architecture and preserved the national style of Chinese architecture. Seven buildings were completed in 1932, including the Conference Building 100, the Science Museum 200, the Literature Museum 300, and the office buildings and student dormitories from 400 to 700. In 1934, the library and the auditorium were built, forming an architectural complex in a distinctive "Chinese-and-Western" style. Today, the Suiyuan campus of Nanjing Normal University basically keeps its original architectural appearance and it enjoys a reputation of "the most beautiful campus in the East".

The Literati's Mettle

When it comes to education in Nanjing, these familiar names must be mentioned, Cai Yuanpei, Hu Shi, Zhang Henshui, Liang Shiqiu, Tao Xingzhi, Yu Pingbo, etc. These men of the Republic of China possessed both Chinese and Western learning, capability, perseverance, patriotism and caring for the people, which formed the character of the literati of the Republic of China. At the time of the transition between the old and the new culture, they educated people, wrote books and carried out educational reforms. Cai Yuanpei, "the academic guru", served as the president of the Academia Sinica for 13 years in Nanjing. His most prominent contribution to modern education in China was more than his clear opposition to the feudal education system and his educational policy of "morality, intelligence, physical fitness, and aesthetics". Others' contributions were the "spirit of independence and the thought of freedom" pursued by Chen Yinke, "Cawing like crows to die rather than living in silence" abided by Hu Shi, Tao Xingzhi's perseverance in saving the country through education, and patriotic writer Zhang Henshui's "How can I fear to die if the country needs me"... These men of Republic of China strode with enthusiasm, and they had prepared democracy and freedom for people in thought.

The culture industry apparently reflected the spirit of the Nanjing citizens. Journalism was booming during that period. In 1932, Nanjing had 29 registered daily newspaper offices, 48 news agencies, 36 magazine offices, and 2 Chinese-Western newspaper offices. The development of journalism in the Republic of China was closely related to the progress of society and education of Nanjing. In particular, new intellectuals stepped

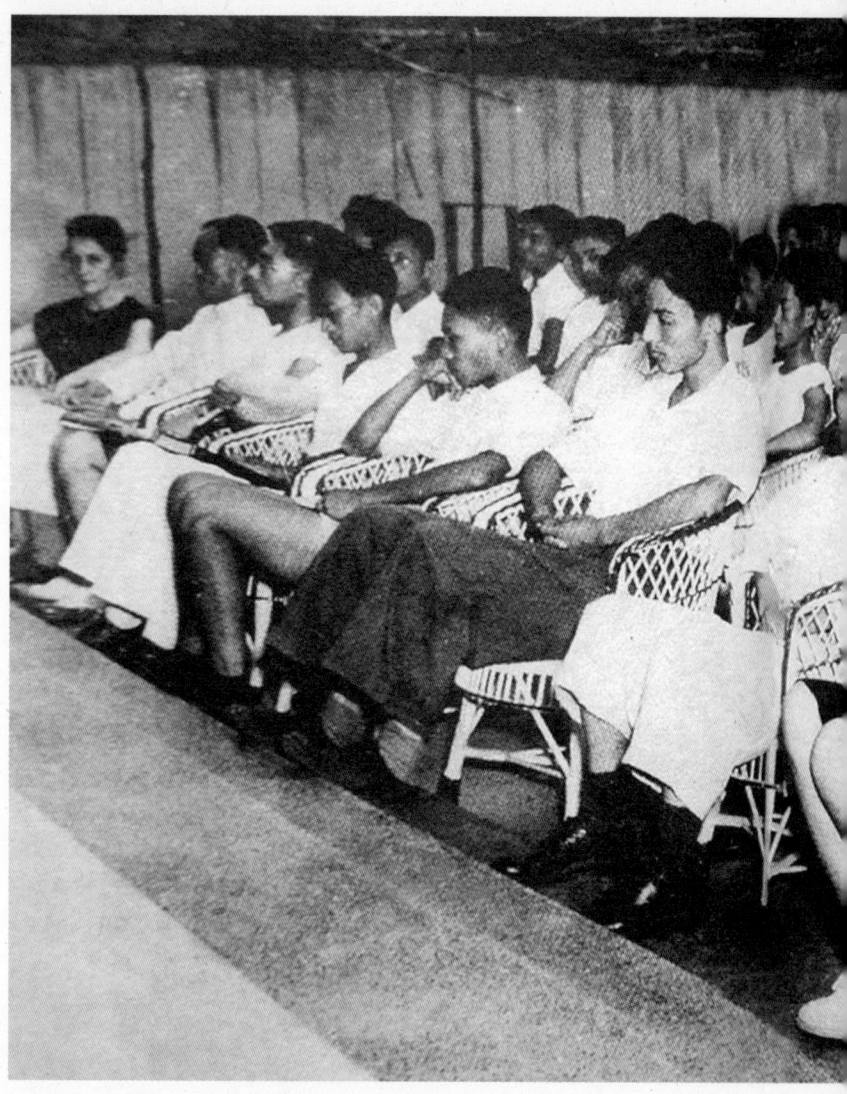

Fig.1-37 Nanjing Youths Attending a Foreign Concert

onto the political arena, and the increasing income of the urban citizens was a market-driven factor of the development of journalism. News media played an important role in building the civilization of the society, and also reflected the social vitality.

At that time, the youth began to receive Western culture and actively participated in cultural and sports activities, such as song-and-dance competitions and concerts. Women became fashionable; especially wearing cheongsam and high-heeled shoes was popular among them in the new era. Product advertisements mostly showed the women's popular clothing, hairstyles and makeup, some in Western style and others in the national style. They led the fashion trend, which also reflected the freedom, openness and comfort of the women's life in Nanjing.

Fig.1-38 Fashionable Nanjing Young Women

During that period, adhering to the concept that "the renewal of the national status and spirit depends on the people's sound physique", Nanjing also actively promoted sports program, which played an irreplaceable role especially in the modern history of the Olympic Games in China. The Chinese Olympic Committee in the Republic of China was established in the chemistry lab of Southeast University. The first National Games of modern China was held in Nanjing Racecourse. The office of the Chinese Olympic Committee in the Republic of China was settled at No. 7 Jian'ge Road. Song Ruhai, the first Chinese who attended the Olympic Games, graduated from Jinling University. Nanjing was the birthplace of China's Olympic dream and it was the pioneer of modern sports in China. In 1930, the government of the city decided to build the Central Stadium [Fig.1-39], the largest stadium in the country, for the Fifth National Games. The main construction of the Central Stadium was the track and field stadium, also including swimming pools, tennis courts, basketball courts (also used as volleyball courts), Chinese martial arts courts, football fields and other parts. The stands in all courts could accommodate more than 60,000 spectators. During the same period, sports such as swimming, cycling, and even golf also emerged in Nanjing. As the capital city, Nanjing attracted various countries to come to find sites for embassies. The diplomats also introduced golf here, which gradually played an important role in the social communication for Chinese and foreign people.

Fig.1-39 The Central Stadium during the Republic of China

After continuous construction for over ten years, Nanjing initially turned out to be a modern city. At that time, it was not only a national city but also a global one, peaceful and romantic. The urban spirit and peace were reflected everywhere through the city planning, architecture, culture, and civilians. It included the convergence of cultures from all countries in the form of openness and peace, with a beautiful vision for the stability and harmony in the future. However, its move to prosperity was ruthlessly stopped by the outbreak of the war, and the deepest and most brutal traumatic memory of Nanjing started.

Sports, You Are Peace!

Sports and peace are inseparable. Coubertin, "father of the modern Olympics" as well as French sports educator, said in his *Ode to Sports*, "Ah, sports, you are peace!" His famous saying "I summon the youth of the world to compete on the sports field, instead of fighting on the battlefield", which became the peace creed of the modern Olympics. The Olympic spirit formulated by the "Olympic Charter" is "mutual understanding, long-term friendship, solidarity and fair competition". The Olympic motto of "Faster, Higher, Stronger—Together" not only means to go all out and challenge oneself in competitive sports, but also signifies the ideal of national prosperity and rejuvenation. Sport is a world language, and it transcends the boundaries of nations, religions, and cultures. It not only demonstrates the positive and active spirit of a country and a city, but also conveys the common aspiration of peace, friendship and unity of mankind.

2

Chapter 2

Defending Peace against Atrocities

On July 7, 1937, the Japanese War of Aggression against China broke out on a full scale after the "Lugouqiao Incident" (also the "Marco Polo Bridge Incident"). On December 1, 1937, the Japanese base camp issued an order to capture Nanjing [Fig.2-1], and it fell on December 13. Bloody terrifying atrocities occurred, corpses scattering all around. Nanjing, the former prosperous ancient capital, was devastated and became a "hell on earth".

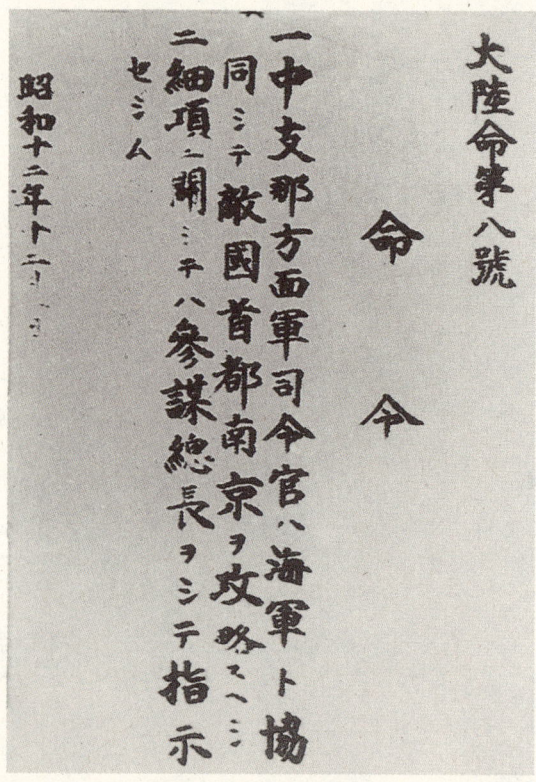

Fig.2-1 The Order to Capture Nanjing Issued by the Japanese Base Camp

Resistance in the Dark

Nanjing under the Brutality

The entire city was engulfed with bloody killings from the first day the Japanese troops occupied Nanjing. The Japanese army initially claimed that they only eliminated those Chinese soldiers who were disguised among the civilians, but they had never intended to make a careful distinction at all. During those days, the rifle shooting always sounded over and over again. Tilman Duding, a reporter of *New York Times*, saw 200 Chinese men killed on the riverside road, and the whole process took only ten minutes. The city of Nanjing, which was thriving before, suddenly became strange and terrifying. The citizens were afraid to go out and could not lead a normal life.

Fig.2-2 The Japanese Invaders Occupied Nanjing City

The Japanese troops unceasingly hunted and slaughtered for many days, turning Nanjing into a veritable "slaughterhouse". The number of victims constantly rose, and the scenes of suffering and misery could be seen everywhere. Numerous women were raped and killed, and their remains were thrown away or burned all around. Their family members would be killed immediately if any resistance from them was found.

Georg Rosen, the German ambassador to China, mentioned in a telegram to the German Foreign Office on March 4, 1938 that the Japanese soldiers practiced bayoneting unarmed living people. For example, a woman was thrust in the back with a bayonet, the point of which came out of her chest. She was sent to the American Mission Hospital and died there five minutes later.

The women who survived endured both physical and mental torture. Some lost their dear family members, and some lost their chance to be a mother forever. At the age of flowers, they should have enjoyed the sunshine and have a bright future, but were going to death in the brutal tortures. The Japanese troops also forcibly conscripted Chinese women as sex slaves. The Sex Slave ("comfort women") System started in Shanghai in early 1932, but Nanjing was one of the cities with the largest number of comfort stations and "comfort women" in Asia. The women who were snatched or deceived by the Japanese were imprisoned in comfort stations everywhere, and were insulted and tortured by the Japanese soldiers. Even for the survivors who escaped, this unbearable experience brought great humiliation and pain to their lives, and completely changed their life.

Lei Guiying was one of them, her father died when she was young and her mother remarried. In August 1941, the helpless girl applied for the job after learning the recruitment by the Japanese army, but was tricked into sexual service out of her expectation. Although she was only 13 years old, she was forced to provide sexual service to the Japanese soldiers, and often got beaten and tortured. She realized that death turned out to be so "easy". Of the fourteen girls she first went there with, only six survived after a year and a half, and the rest were all tortured to death. Finally one day, Lei Guiying took advantage of the evening darkness and succeeded escaping from the toilet at the back door. But even after leaving the "hell on earth", she could not lead a normal life. Besides the mental injury, the old woman had a scar on the head by the gun butt, and a leg wound over ten centimeters long made by the Japanese soldier. She walked limp, and was disabled for life. She also lost her reproductive function and had no choice but adopt two children.

In 2006, Lei Guiying was inspired by Park Young-Shim, a "comfort woman" from North Korean, who came to Nanjing to identify the site of the former comfort station, and decided to publicly testify against the Japanese crimes of comfort women's policy to the media and provided her testimony and physical evidence to the historians. She donated a bottle of potassium permanganate disinfectant powder [Fig.2-3] that was given to "comfort women" by the comfort station to wash their sexual organs, and identified the exact addresses of the two former comfort stations in Nanjing. Her behavior was a great self-challenge for those who used to be "comfort women", because only a few survivors were willing to talk about what they had gone through. They were afraid to look back on their pain, and to be the target of humiliation and ridicule from the outside world, which would disrupt their peaceful life again. The survivors of "comfort women", affected by the traditional concept of chastity in Asia, would choose to keep silent.

Fig.2-3 **Potassium Permanganate Disinfection Powder Distributed by the Japanese Army to Lei Guiying**

According to Hsienli Tan's study, there were five former "comfort women" who hoped to give testimony only behind the curtains and with their feet exposed to the public. This deep-rooted ethical complex made it quite difficult to reveal the historical truth.

In April 2007, Lei Guiying died at the age of 79 in Nanjing. In her last will and testament, the old woman expressed her initial intention, "I bravely stood up this time, not for some money (compensation), but for justice and for the tens of thousands of compatriots killed by the Japanese imperialists… The Chinese people and the others in the world shall never forget the devastating disaster in the history though it has passed for more than sixty years. In the era of peace, each of us Chinese and people of all countries must learn from history, and remember this evil period. I hope that this tragedy will not happen again, and there will be no more wars. War is evil."

The appalling atrocities the Japanese army committed during the war constituted the most vivid mnemonics in the narrative of the Nanjing Massacre. These symbols, evolved into "synonyms" of war and violence, and death and suffering, acting as a "catalyst" to consolidate the memories of the victims, have left unforgettable collective trauma to the Chinese people, as well as an indelible historical imprint on everyone's individual consciousness. People in Nanjing at this moment yearned for peace, and their desire to oppose war became even stronger. The Chinese military, civilians and international friends formed a force of fighting against war and maintaining peace at the critical juncture of national peril. Their mutual help, self-sacrifice, courage and perseverance manifested the boundless love of mankind and the pursuit of justice.

National Salvation

In the huge city of Nanjing, the departing from the family and death occurred every day. Numerous heroes stood out, bearing their nation and faith in mind, and performing countless touching and admirable deeds. Regardless of their own lives, they firmly pursued justice in their hearts, and fought bravely for peace.

When the Japanese troops were shooting at the captured Chinese soldiers and civilians along the Caoxiexia River, these people, shouting "Wrest the gun! Take the gun!" despite the Japanese machine guns, rushed towards the Japanese soldiers with their bare hands until all fell down and died. Many civilians had never held a gun or known how to avoid bullets, but they chose to die.

In 1939, the event of "toxic liquor" made a stir in the city. Brothers Zhan Changbing and Zhan Changlin, servants in the Japanese Consulate General in Nanjing, risked putting the poison into the liquor that the high-ranking Japanese and the puppet officials were drinking, killing and harming several Japanese military and political leaders. Afterwards, the Zhan brothers wrote an open letter to the Japanese Consul General angrily denouncing the atrocities committed by the Japanese army in Nanjing, and saying, "Since we have done it, we are not afraid of death. If we were caught, we would like to help those victims revenge and die without regrets!" Their heroic deeds showed the brave and fearless national spirit and responsibility.

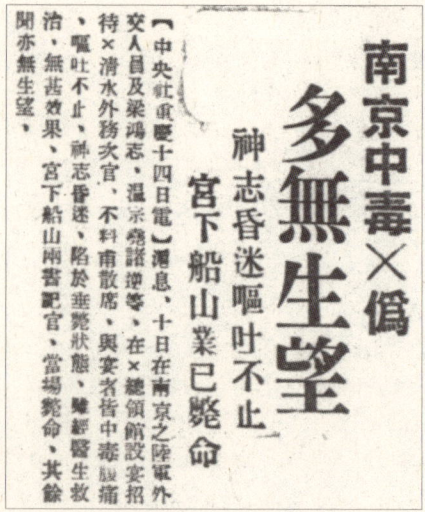

Fig.2-4 The Report on the "Toxic Liquor Event" in *Shun Pao* (Hong Kong, 1939)

After the Japanese army occupied the city, both the Kuomintang and the Communist Party established secret underground organizations in Nanjing. The Communist Party of China successively established a special branch and Nanjing Working Committee there. The New Fourth Army arrived at the battlefield behind the enemy lines in southern Jiangsu in May 1938. They were active in various places in Nanjing for a long time and fought fiercely with the puppet troops on Jutang Highway, Lukou, Chishan, Jinniu Mountain, Babaiqiao, and Guabu. The Kuomintang also established a secret party headquarter in Nanjing. The National Government Military Committee sent troops to fight the Japanese and puppet troops outside Nanjing.

In 1940, the Japanese army built two concentration camps in the riverside area around Sanjing Dock. The concentration camp was surrounded by water on three sides. Around it, three two-meter-high barbed wire fences were erected, in the middle of which was a live wire, and the exit was under the guard of the blockhouse. From the spring of 1941, the Japanese army escorted the captured Chinese people, including the officers and soldiers of Kuomintang, of New Fourth Army and guerrilla from Taiyuan, Beijing, Shanghai, Wuhan and other places, to the Pukou Concentration Camp in six batches. The living conditions in the camp were harsh, and the captured people lived in the dilapidated wooden houses. A fairly large broken house was crowded in more than a hundred people. When it was windy and rainy outside, the roof was leaking unceasingly. The captured Chinese were given moldy food in the concentration camp, only a bowl of rice for each meal, while they had to do heavy manual labor under the armed supervision of the Japanese soldiers. It was not uncommon for the captured people to get sick and die. However, many of them held the determination of "I would rather die than be a subjugated slave" and refused to go to work. They would rather commit suicide than do any good to the Japanese army.

The oppression and insults from the Japanese army aroused the anger of the captured soldiers and civilians. Despite the extreme conditions, they successively organized four riots in the Pukou Concentration Camp. In a riot, they brandished wooden sticks and shovels killing several Japanese soldiers, rushed out of the camp gates, and ran along the railway embankment. They were about to run out of this "cage", when a train happened to come from the opposite direction, blocking their way. Unfortunately, they were arrested, and hundreds of them were killed by the Japanese troops who were chasing them up. By the time the Japanese surrendered, the survivors were only 800 out of the 5,000 odd captured people. More than 4,000 were killed because of their involvement in the riots or were tortured to death in the concentration camp.

After the victory of the War of Resistance against Japanese Aggression, the Kuomintang government built the "Memorial Tower for the Victims of the War of Resistance against Japanese Aggression" and a monument in order to commemorate the officers and soldiers who died in the Pukou Concentration Camp. On October 26, 1947, the Kuomintang government sent important officials to preside over the memorial meeting and held a solemn inauguration ceremony. However, it was destroyed in 1954. In 1989, the Nanjing Municipal People's Government decided to rebuild a monument to the Victims of the Officials and Soldiers in the War of Resistance against Japanese Aggression in Pukou District. The front of the stele was engraved with nine Chinese characters, "Monument to Official-and-Soldier Victims in War of Resistance against Japanese Aggression", and on the back was the inscription written by the People's Government of Pukou District of Nanjing City in memory of the deceased. The top of the monument was shaped like a clenched fist, demonstrating the heroic spirit of fighting to the end and preferring death to surrender.

Civil Non-Violent Resistance

After the Japanese took over Nanjing, they followed the plans to "use China to control China", "use war to support war", and enslave the minds of the people in the occupied area. No weapons in hand and unable to withstand gun attacks, Nanjing citizens did not give up hope, but adopted a non-violent strategy to resist and to defend peace. Resistance did not necessarily have to be confrontation, while non-violence was also a powerful force.

The workers in Nanjing chose "sabotage" strategy to deal with the Japanese occupation. As an old factory in Nanjing, there were more than 10,000 Chinese workers in Puzhen Machinery Factory. After it was taken over by the Japanese army, the workers dilly-dallied and made poor repairs when the machine was broken. The Xiaguan Power Plant, a key department, was also taken over by the Japanese army and the workers deliberately hindered its normal operation, such as load reduction, boiler flameout, shutdown, and power cuts; or burning more coal, wasting the Japanese military strategic materials; going on strike in the power station, etc. They were severely suppressed and punished by the Japanese army, but they did not give in, and instead adopted a more concealed way to create serious production accidents. This kind of struggle continued until the victory of the war.

The education sector in Nanjing also joined the non-cooperative resistance. After the fall of Nanjing, the Japanese army tried every means to implement "enslavement" education policy, in an attempt to discourage the residents from resisting, but their obscurantism was resolutely objected by the teachers, students and parents in Nanjing. Some teachers would rather be unemployed than teach under the Japanese puppet government. Some parents would rather send their children to private schools for education than go to the Japanese puppet public schools. During that period, the teachers took various opportunities to encourage students to learn the language, history and geography of their motherland, and cultivate students' patriotism. The students spontaneously organized salvation groups and patriotic movements against Japanese aggression to actively promote patriotism. In the spring of 1942, students of Nanjing Central University, such as Zhuang Peilin, Huang Guibin, and Rui Qinhe, established a "civil society" among their classmates, to make friends, contact the masses, and admit potential revolutionaries by holding activities, like writing poetry, outings, and evening parties. The students of the education college also spontaneously organized the "Central University Branch of China Salvation Congress" to promote patriotic thoughts.

Under the Japanese brutality, the Nanjing military and civilians fought back and protected peace in their own ways. They were all ordinary people, ordinary but extraordinary, demonstrating the Chinese spirit of unyieldingness and national unity. Perhaps the sudden holocaust brought them more panic, fear and helplessness, but they were not at the mercy of others. Though unarmed, they bravely chose ceaseless struggle and even sacrificed their precious lives. Every silent resistance was a declaration of those unyielding people.

The Light of Peace in the Wartime

After the fall of Nanjing, the embassies of foreign countries evacuated their overseas residents who were working or doing business in China. British and American journalists were also required to evacuate for their safety. The capital city was temporarily reduced to a "slaughterhouse on earth" isolated from the rest of the world. At this time, 24 foreigners voluntarily remained to stay in Nanjing. They could have stayed aside during the cruel war, or left safely under the arrangement of their governments, but they did not hesitate to remain there. They did their best to protect the Chinese refugees although it's far beyond their capability to stop the atrocities committed by the Japanese army. A buffer wall was built between the Japanese army and the unarmed Chinese civilians, giving so many Chinese refugees hope of survival. They were not only selfless guardians of the refugees, but also recorders and witnesses of the war atrocities. They kept a lot of letters, diaries, and video materials during the Nanjing Massacre, which mostly involved the atrocities of the Japanese military they had witnessed, and recorded this unprecedented human tragedy in an accurate manner. Their deeds showed international humanitarianism and admirable dedication and courage in this dehumanizing war. Their names would be kept forever in the minds of the Chinese people, and they were also the light of peace in the wartime.

International Rescue of Nanjing

These 24 foreigners who stayed in Nanjing during the massacre included John Rabe, Miner Bates, Wilson Mills, George Fitch, Hubert Sone (Chinese name Song Xubo), John Magee, James McCallum (Chinese name Maikelun), Minnie Vautrin (Chinese name Hua Qun), Lewis Smythe, Eduard Sperling and Robert Wilson, and so on. They came from churches, schools, government agencies, hospitals, news media and other institutions or companies in Nanjing, and took every means to participate in or organize rescue of the refugees, the wounded and sick civilians. Some of them even gave their precious lives to help the Chinese people fight for freedom and peace. This is known as "International Rescue of Nanjing" in history.

Good Man of Nanjing: John Rabe

John Rabe was born in Hamburg, Germany. He was sent to China by Siemens Company and did business in Beijing, Tianjin, Nanjing and other cities. Before he moved to No.1 Xiaofenqiao of Nanjing, he had lived in China for more than 20 years and had deep feelings for this country. Not long before the Japanese invasion of Nanjing in 1937, Rabe, a manager of Siemens' Nanjing branch, and the company's foreign employees were told by Trautmann the German ambassador to China to evacuate Nanjing quickly, but Rabe refused and said, "Many institutions, factories and hospitals in Nanjing are all using Siemens products, and Siemens shall be responsible for their maintenance. We can't leave the job without authorization." He and his family used to have a happy life in China, with his children and grandchildren also born here. If he was forced to leave China in this most critical moment, his conscience would be condemned, and it was not in conformity to Christian ethics.

What if They Were Our Fellow Countrymen?

Rabe wrote in his diary, "Times are bitterly hard here in the country of my hosts, who have treated me well for three decades now. The rich are fleeing, the poor must stay behind. They don't know where to go. They don't have the means to flee. Aren't they in danger of being slaughtered in great numbers? Shouldn't one make an attempt to help them? Save a few at least! What if they were our fellow countrymen?"

In the end, Rabe decided to take the risk to remain in Nanjing, and then co-sponsored the establishment of the Nanking Safety Zone with more than 20 other foreigners. This organization protected about 250,000 refugees during the massacre. In his own house and small garden, he also successfully protected more than 600 Chinese refugees. He was elected as the Chairman of the International Committee for the Nanking Safety Zone, so besides his business of the branch office, he embarked on the resettlement of the refugees: rearranging air-raid shelters, taking care of the refugees' meals and living, negotiating and mediating with the Japanese military, demonstrating his great love of life, and pursuit of justice in China. In order to express the gratitude to him, the residents of Nanjing respected him as "the Living Buddha of Nanjing", "Good Man of Nanjing", "Oskar Schindler of China".

Fig.2-5 Group Photo of John Rabe (in the Middle) outside the Headquarters of Nanking Safety Zone Committee in 1938

Rabe was ordered to leave Nanjing and return to Germany by Siemens headquarters at the end of January 1938. After returning to Germany, he continued to publicize, hold report meetings, and submit written reports to the German authorities to expose the atrocities committed by the Japanese in Nanjing. *Rabe's Diary*, which he wrote during the war, was dedicated to the world by Mrs. Ursula Reinhardt, Rabe's granddaughter, and published in China in 1996. There were 20 volumes of *Rabe's Diary*, among which 10 were about the Nanjing Massacre, with more than 2,400 pages. They are one of the most important and detailed historical records of the Nanjing Massacre currently preserved by a third party. Turning over *Rabe's Diary*, you can read various touching details besides the description of the atrocities in the war: for example, whenever a Japanese air raid began, Rabe would open the door to have people enter the air-raid shelter for refuge. There was a Chinese-German bilingual notice at the entrance of the cave, stipulating that children and women occupied the middle position because it was the safest place; men used the seats on both sides or stood. Rabe would stand outside, leaving safety to others but danger to himself.

Chinese People Will Never Forget You

Rabe was in a bleak situation after he returned to Germany. After learning the news, the citizens of Nanjing specially organized a fundraiser for him and mailed him a large amount of food and goods. He was buried in the cemetery of the Kaiser Wilhelm Memorial Church after his death in Berlin in 1950. In 1985, the management department removed his tombstone because the lease of the cemetery expired and no one renewed the lease. The Chinese side had negotiated with the city of Berlin, hoping to keep this place as a historical relic, but was rejected. Finally, in 2013 funded by the Nanjing Municipal People's Government and with the help of the Chinese Embassy in Germany, the Rabe Cemetery [Fig.2-6] was rebuilt on the original site of Rabe's tombstone to express the Chinese people's infinite gratitude and miss for his humanitarian actions.

Fig.2-6 Rabe Cemetery

Debunker of the Massacre: Miner Bates

Miner Bates, a historian, once pursued his studies at Oxford, Yale and other prestigious universities. During the massacre, he served as a professor, head of the History Department, dean of the Faculty of Arts, and vice president of Jinling University. As a scholar who studied Eastern history and believed in Christian pacifism, he had deep feelings for the histories and cultures of China and Japan, and he did not favor either side subjectively. He always called on the two peoples to live in friendship and strengthen economic and cultural exchanges. During the Nanjing Massacre, as the pivot of the Nanking Safety Zone Committee, he was under tremendous pressure to save the lives of more innocent civilians. Despite adversity, he did not give up without a struggle. At that time, Bates was alone in Nanjing, while his wife and children were stranded in Japan. In a letter to his wife, he said, "I have been struggling in pain in order to establish a safety zone for the civilians and refugees hosted by international figures. There are some chances of success."

Bates was heartbroken when he saw the former prosperous Nanjing being looted and burnt unscrupulously. For this reason, he wrote to the Japanese embassy more than once as the Chairman of the International Committee for the Nanking Safety Zone to protest the war crimes committed by the Japanese army. At the same time, Bates also constantly wrote letters to the US embassy, accusing the Japanese military of what they had done, and especially emphasized their acts that violated US interests, in hope that the Unite States could come forward to mediate. Bates made a large number of documentary reports in historian style on the wartime situation. After the war, Bates attended the International Military Tribunal for the Far East to testify against the Japanese military. The main historical materials left by him are currently stored in the special collections reading room at the Yale Divinity Library in the "Miner Searle Bates Papers" archives, which have become precious first-hand historical materials documenting the Nanjing Massacre.

Yale Collections

In 1946, Mr. Zhang Kaiyuan went to study at the History Department of Jinling University. He was greatly influenced by Bates, who served as the university professor then, and the two had an unforgettable teacher-student relationship. In 1987, Zhang Kaiyuan was president and professor of History Department at Central China Normal University. He went to search for research materials at Yale Divinity Library, and unexpectedly discovered the original materials kept about the Nanjing Massacre written by his instructor Bates. Although this was not his research field at the time, he began to collect relevant materials and compiled them into a book in order to restore the truth of that period of history. As soon as these books were published, they were queried by the Japanese right-wing forces, saying that the "Bates Papers" were only his personal account, not very much convincing. To this end, Zhang Kaiyuan once again went to the Yale Divinity Library and found the original materials left by those members of the International Committee for the Nanking Safety Zone at that time, including George Fitch, Ernest Forster, John Magee, Robert Wilson, and Minnie Vautrin. These historical materials are collectively referred to as the "Yale Collections", and they have also become the first-hand materials that confirm the authenticity of that period of history.

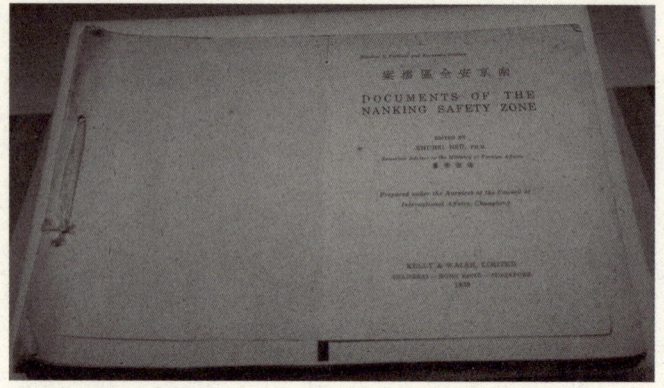

Fig.2-7 A Copy of Documents of the Nanking Safety Zone from Yale Collections

"In the Service of Peace": George Fitch

George Fitch, son of a missionary couple, was born in Suzhou, and his Chinese name was Fei Wusheng. After graduating from Columbia University, he was sent to China again as an instructor of the Young Men's Christian Association (YMCA). During the War of Resistance against Japanese Aggression, Fitch served as the head of the YMCA Nanjing Branch, a close comrade of John Rabe, and later director-general of the international committee. He was proficient in Chinese and knew many military and political officials of the National Government. Therefore, he was responsible for negotiating food and funding with the government personnel, and raising relief funds from Shanghai Christian groups and charities. He took the risk of sending the films taken by John Magee to Shanghai by sewing them into the lining of his camel-hair coat. Once discovered by the Japanese soldiers, Fitch might be in great danger. When he arrived in Shanghai, he immediately rushed to Kodak, edited and copied the film with Harold John Timperley, a reporter of the British *Manchester Guardian* in Shanghai, and began to spread the terrible atrocities committed by the Japanese army in Nanjing. Later, Fitch delivered speeches in Washington DC, New York, Los Angeles, Hawaii and other cities, telling about the atrocities taking place in

Nanjing, and won foreign support for Chinese Resistance against the Japanese Aggression. At the same time, he himself wrote in his diaries the atrocities of the Japanese army. These personal statements and written materials were important evidences in the Tokyo Trials.

The Fitches had deep feelings for China. He loved the Chinese like he loved himself. When he was badly needed by the Chinese, he chose to come forward. Looking back on his life, Fitch said, "I was born in China… so China has become my second hometown. When I serve in China, I am also serving my motherland, and at the same time working for human justice, democracy and peace."

Guardian Angel: Minnie Vautrin

Minnie Vautrin came to China in September 1919 to serve as the acting dean of Jinling Women's College of Arts and Sciences after she had received a master's degree from the Teachers College of Columbia University. During the Nanjing Massacre, she was the head of the refugee camp at Jinling Women's College of Arts and Sciences. She guarded the gate of the college most of the day to prevent Japanese troops from entering the campus. At her invitation, a male American missionary would come to help guard the campus every night and she also arranged staff to patrol the campus day and night. When she heard that the Japanese soldiers were looking for "flower girls" from house to house, she took the risk of accepting hundreds of women and children into the camp at Jinling Women's College of Arts and Sciences, which incurred the anger of the Japanese troops. However, facing the threat of the bayonet and intimidation of violence, she still tenaciously protected the Chinese women and children.

Fig.2-8 Group Photo of Some Staff in the Refugee Camp of Jinling Women's College of Arts and Sciences (the Sixth from the Left is Vautrin)

Fig.2-9 Refugees Lining up to Be Vaccinated

In order to help the refugees, Vautrin did everything possible to raise funds and life supplies. She took out the food from the school and distributed it to the refugees. The Red Cross Porridge Plant provided the refugees with rice porridge twice a day. There was also a small clinic in the college, which was run by Mrs. Cheng, who was Vautrin's colleague and assistant. They also distributed milk powder and nutrition products to infants and young children in the refugee camps on a regular basis, and assisted in vaccinating thousands of refugees, in addition to providing basic medical assistance and medicine to the refugees and teaching women something about public health and personal hygiene.

Vautrin and her colleagues collected thousands of identification information and petitions, and helped the women in the camps find their separated family members, even though most of those lost might have been killed in such a turbulent environment. In order to enable those women to have a life skill, Vautrin also organized some housekeeping and skill training classes to teach sewing, poultry breeding, etc., hoping that they could live a normal life after the war. As a third-party witness of this war, Vautrin, regardless of the dangerous environment, insisted on keeping a diary to write down what she had seen and heard almost every day. The *Vautrin's Diary* written by her had a total of more than 500,000 words, with smooth writing and delicate emotions, which left later generations with evidence of close perception and reflection on the war.

I Cannot Put aside China at this Time!

On December 1, 1937, the US Embassy called together all US citizens who stranded in Nanjing for the last time, and warned, "If you don't evacuate, we will not be able to guarantee your safety in the future." Vautrin said firmly again, "I can't put aside China at this time!" Regardless of her personal safety, she signed the certificate that "I won't leave Nanjing in any case" presented by the embassy. This was the fourth time that she solemnly rejected the request of the US Embassy to leave Nanjing. Vautrin, who remained in Nanjing, protected tens of thousands of women. Many people admired her for her bravery, fearlessness and love. Mr. Rabe vividly praised Ms. Vautrin in his diary, she was "protecting them like brooding hens caring for chicks".

The Photographer Who Revealed the Truth: John Magee

John Magee was sent to China by the Anglican Church in America (ACA) as a priest in 1912. After arriving in China, he worked as a missionary in the Nanjing Daosheng Church run by the ACA. During the Nanjing Massacre, Magee served as the Chairman of the Nanjing Branch of the International Red Cross and a member of the International Committee for the Nanking Safety Zone. He also participated in diagnosis, treatment and rescue work at Drum Tower Hospital. He risked his life preserving the visual evidence of the Nanjing atrocities. The films were brought out of Nanjing by George Fitch, his companion, giving the world a chance to understand the human tragedy that Nanjing was going through.

Fig.2-10 John Magee (Center of the First Row) with Staff and Patients at Drum Tower Hospital (Summer 1938)

   This film was shot by John Magee between December 1937 and January 1938, altogether in 8 reels. The total length of the existing film was 105 minutes, and it was the only motion pictures about the Nanjing Massacre. Magee said frankly, "what we had seen and heard was only a fraction of the atrocities that took place in this city, but I thought this was enough to give you an understanding of the hellish experiences that people had gone through in this city." In the introduction of the film, he also wrote down the purpose of shooting the film, "(I) recorded these scenes not to incite revenge against Japan, but just to hope that all people, including the Japanese, should keep in mind the terrible consequences of this war and understand that all legal

Fig.2-11 The Camera and Films used by John Magee to Film the Atrocities of the Japanese Army

means should be used to end this conflict provoked by the Japanese military." Eight years later, in 1946, Magee's film was employed as the video evidence for the accusation of the Japanese atrocities in Nanjing at the International Military Tribunal for the Far East.

The Japanese military carried out a schemed blockade on the news of Nanjing in the war. They destroyed the original Chinese news media organizations in the city, and cut off all telecommunication links between Nanjing and the outside world. They did not want the outside world to know anything about Nanjing. This also explained why the original reports on the massacre were almost entirely reprinted from the Western media. It was the Western journalists who remained in Nanjing at that time risking their lives recording and reporting the atrocities committed by the Japanese army that allowed the news of these atrocities to spread throughout China and even to the world through various channels, causing more people to be aware of the cruelty of the war, and also exerting pressure on Japan to end the war as soon as possible.

The Benevolent Doctor: Robert Wilson

Robert Wilson grew up in Nanjing, so he had a special affection for this city. In 1936, he returned to Nanjing with his family after he had completed his studies in the United States and worked as a surgeon in Drum Tower Hospital. Before the fall of Nanjing, the American Embassy urged the Americans to evacuate for many times, but Wilson decided to remain in Nanjing. He was the "only surgeon in Nanjing" except the Japanese military surgeons before 1938. During the massacre, Wilson treated countless patients and made them feel the warmth of humanity. In addition to rescuing the dying and the injured, he also served as the hospital driver and joined the Nanjing Branch of the International Red Cross to assist the International Committee for the Nanking Safety Zone to protect the refugees in Nanking. He also submitted evidence of Japanese atrocities to the Japanese side, and initiated joint protests against them.

At that time, the Drum Tower Hospital was responsible for treating the wounded refugees. However, the director Tan Hedun (John Horton Daniels) and most Chinese and foreign medical staff were forced to evacuate Nanjing when the Japanese army aggressively attacked Nanjing in the end of November 1937. Only a total of over 20 people remained there, like James McCallum, a missionary who took over as the director temporarily, Robert Wilson, surgeon, C. S. Trimmer, physician, Grace Bauer, chemist and nurse, and I. Hynds, nurse, some American and Chinese medical staff. As the only hospital open to the citizens at that time, Drum Tower Hospital received a large number of patients, though it was struggling to run because of extreme shortage of money and manpower, and the bad conditions of Japanese military intrusions. They were not afraid of hardships, risking and being overworked in hospital to treat the wounded civilians. For thousands of the wounded refugees, such a rescue force was like a small boat to an isolated island carrying the hope of life and composing a song of life.

A Bleakest City of Nanjing

Dr. Wilson wrote in his diary on December 18, 1937: "After checking the 150 patients under my care, I left the hospital and went back to dinner. A full moon rose slowly from Purple Mountain, and the night was so beautiful that it was beyond description. But at the time being, the city of Nanjing in the moonlight was the bleakest and the most desolate since the Taiping Heavenly Kingdom. The nine-tenths of the city was abandoned, and in the remaining one-tenth area crowded nearly 200,000 frightened refugees. The Japanese soldiers were roaming the streets and looting everywhere… Refugees would face hunger in the near future, and there would be no fuel for winter… This was not a pleasant winter we expected…"

Besides Drum Tower Hospital, the International Red Cross also set up two clinics. The Nanjing Branch of the Red Cross and some international Red Cross members acted together to provide a large amount of selfless assistance to the victims and refugees, including getting together burial teams, offering porridge, and providing free consultations for the refugees. Although the conditions during the war were hard and resources were extremely scarce and it was necessary to take precautions against the Japanese sudden bomb attacks from time to time, these medical staff selflessly protected the Chinese military and civilians, carried forward the medical professionalism, and fully demonstrated the great spirit of humanism and love.

Shelter in Disaster

In the dark year of 1937, the foreigners who remained in Nanjing formed the "International Committee for the Nanking Safety Zone" spontaneously based on an international humanitarian standpoint in hope of winning more living space for the innocent civilians in the war by virtue of their neutral status as a third party. Their bravery and justice made helpless refugees feel the warmth and brilliance of human nature.

At the end of 1937, Dr. Hang Liwu, Chairman of the Board of Directors of Jinling University and director general of the Sino-English Education Foundation, in view of the situation of the war in China, was inspired by the operation of Rao Jiaju (Robert Jacquinot de Besange, S.J.), a French priest in Shanghai, who set up a refugee area in Shanghai, and called on the Western expatriates who remained here to establish a safety zone to protect the refugees in Nanjing. At first, he gathered around ten or twenty foreigners in Nanjing and proposed to

Fig.2-12 Members of the International Committee for the Nanking Safety Zone (From left to right: Ernest Forster, Wilson Mills, John Rabe, Lewis Smythe, Eduard Sperling, George Fitch)

establish a refugee area, and unexpectedly, most of them agreed to his proposal because it was a humane thing, and Rabe was among them. He wrote in his diary, "Every time the sirens sounded, a large number of poor residents (men, women and children) ran past my house to Wutaishan, where there were some larger air-raid shelters under the mound. In this disaster of Nanjing, I really didn't want to see such a painful sight, not to mention the women holding very young children in their arms." The continuous bombing by Japanese planes outside had left many citizens homeless. The life and death caused by the war were staged in this city every day. Although they didn't know what the future would be like, their common wish was to provide some aid to the people of Nanjing to help them escape the nightmare of the war.

The International Committee for the Nanking Safety Zone was formally established on November 22, with Rabe as Chairman. The committee consisted of four departments: finance, food, housing, and health, which mainly provided the refugees with security, food, hospitals and sanitation facilities, and was in the charge of the committee members. However, none of the members had received corresponding military training, nor had they held a post in government office: Rabe, businessman, Wilson, doctor, Magee, priest, Smythe and Vautrin, university teachers. Out of respect for life and persevering to justice, they provided rescue and shelter for the citizens who were too late to evacuate during the war.

Fig.2-13 Refugees at Headquarters of Nanjing Safety Zone Committee

However, the completion of establishing the safety zone depended on the attitude of the Japanese military. If the safety zone was not recognized by the Japanese side, its "neutrality" and "security" would be of no use. In order to make the Japanese military to "give the green light" to the safety zone, the committee sent a letter to the US Consulate General in Shanghai through the US Embassy, and it would be forwarded to the Japanese ambassador; at the same time, they invited priest Rao Jiaju, who was experienced in negotiation to discuss with the Japanese authorities. The committee particularly hoped that the Japanese government in view of humanism should not station troops, nor set up military agencies, nor bomb, so as to ensure that the safety zone was respected for its civilian purpose. After several twists and turns, the Japanese military only maintained a tacit attitude in the end. After its establishment, the Nanking Safety Zone occupied an area of about 3.86 square kilometers, which was only 1/8 of the entire urban area. It was bounded by roads on all sides, including Italian and American embassies, Jinling University, Jinling Women's College of Arts and Sciences, Drum Tower Hospital and other institutions. However, it was this patch of land that was condensed with voiceless love, like a candle in the dark, lighting up the hope in the hearts of 250,000 homeless refugees.

A number of refugee camps were also set up in the safety zone to accommodate vulnerable groups such as women, children and the elderly who needed assistance. The campus of Jinling Women's College of Arts and Sciences and Jinling University were the two largest refugee camps, and later developed into 25 camps. As the war went on, the Chinese government's funding for the safety zone was increasingly limited. Despite the brutal war, these Westerners and Chinese people did not give up, and struggled to maintain the safety zone with a fearless spirit of humanism until the end.

Fig.2-14 Jinling University Refugee Camp

    There are no borders to kindness. In the tragic moment of Nanjing, more refugees would have lost their lives without shelters in this disaster. A passing of time will not erase history, and the Chinese people will always remember their good deeds. Today, walking on this piece of land less than 4 square kilometers in Nanjing, the sun is warm and the city is peaceful. The ruins here have been well preserved, and only those imprints left by war are constantly reminding us of the fragility and preciousness of our lives, and the hard-won peace.

The Hard-Fought Victory

Arrival of Justice

When the Pacific War broke out in 1941, China joined the world anti-fascist alliance in the battles. On August 15, 1945, Japan announced its unconditional surrender and the war was finally over! The news of victory spread through radio waves to all parts of China. Men and women, old and young, who had suffered from the war for a long time, were all overjoyed at this exciting news. Only those who had experienced gunfire, and life and death, could better understand the hard-won peace. The cities that had suffered from the war finally regained their lives.

On September 9th, Nanjing took off the dull covering from the flames of war, and changed into festival costumes in order to hold the ceremony for Japan's surrender in China Theater [Fig.2-15]. Inside and outside the venue, careful decorations were made to set off an atmosphere of celebrating victory. On both sides of the asphalt road every 50 meters from the intersection of Huangpu Road to the front of the Central Military Academy auditorium, were flagpoles, painted with blue, white and red stripes, erected with the United Nations flags hung on. At the intersection of Huangpu Road, there was a tall archway made of pine and cypress branches and decorated with the four golden Chinese

Fig.2-15 The Ceremony for Japan's Surrender in China Theater

characters "lü se he ping" (green peace); the top of the archway outside the Central Military Academy was embedded with a huge red "V", symbolizing "victory", below which a line of golden characters were posted—"The venue of the ceremony for Japan's surrender in China Theater". There were no empty seats in the venue. A total of about 1,000 people, such as senior Chinese military and civilian officials, representatives of allied countries, Chinese and foreign journalists, together with staff and guards, attended the surrender ceremony, all waiting to witness the arrival of this important historical moment.

The surrender ceremony was hosted by He Yingqin, commander-in-chief of the army in China Theater. The Japanese military representative Okamura Yasuji, commander-in-chief of the Japanese army in China signed and stamped the Japanese Instrument of Surrender, and He Yingqin signed and stamped it after inspection. Subsequently, He Yingqin announced the withdrawal of the Japanese military representative, who bowed and left the auditorium. After the ceremony, He Yingqin delivered a speech on the radio: Dear compatriots all over the country and people all over the world, the ceremony for Japan's surrender in China Theater was successfully completed in Nanjing. This is one of the most meaningful days in Chinese history, and it is the result of the Chinese nation's arduous resistance. The peace and prosperity of mankind in East Asia and the whole world has also opened a new era! China will embark on the road of peace construction and create the great cause of the rejuvenation of the Chinese nation!

The entire surrender ceremony lasted for only 20 minutes, but it seemed as if a century had passed for the Chinese people to wait for this justice. This was not only the victory of the Nanjing people, of the Chinese people, but also that of the world anti-fascist alliance. As the main Eastern battlefield of the world anti-fascist war, the Chinese people have made significant contributions to the victory.

However, true peace is still a long way off, because peace obtained by force is not a lasting peace. Only when everyone becomes a peace-loving person, can they willingly stay away from war and achieve the ultimate goal of all mankind's wish for peace.

Trial for Peace

On January 19, 1946, eleven allied countries, including China, the Soviet Union, the United States, the United Kingdom, France, the Netherlands and Canada and others organized the International Military Tribunal for the Far East (IMTFE) in Tokyo to deal with Japanese war criminals for their crimes against peace, humanity, and initiating war. The trials [Fig.2-16] lasted for two and a half years with 818 sessions. Their scale was unprecedented, even surpassing the international trials in Nuremberg, making them the largest one in history so far. As for the Japanese war criminals arrested in China, military tribunals in China were set up in Beijing, Nanjing, Shanghai, Hankou, Guangzhou and other cities to conduct trials in order to redress the grievances of the victims and uphold human justice.

In these trials "crimes against peace" were repeatedly mentioned, which showed that any act that undermined human peace and security was clearly identified as an international crime. The crime specifically included "planning, preparation, initiation, or waging of a war of invasion, or of a war in violation of international treaties, agreements or assurances, or participation in a common plan or conspiracy for the accomplishment of any of the foregoing". Joseph Berry Keenan, the chief of Counsel of prosecution in the Tokyo Trials, mentioned "humanity" and "peace" over and over again in his opening statement. He said, "To say that wars of the future will literally threaten the existence, not alone of civilization but of all beings, has become such a truism that its reiteration here seems trite. This problem of peace, which has ever been the desire of the human race, has now reached

Fig.2-16 Tokyo Trials

a position of the crossroads. For the implements of destruction that we already know of, even in what might well be primitive development, have reached such proportions that only the human imagination at its highest development is fit to cope with the realities. Our question at the crossroads is now literally an answer: 'To be or not to be'... What can we do with the powers conferred upon us here in this courtroom to contribute in a just and efficient manner to the prevention of future wars? Every individual's life is sacred and inviolable, and it can never be legally sacrificed for immoral purposes." At this level, what the Tokyo Trials sought was to prevent or deter the war, not for narrow and despicable purposes such as revenge. The ultimate meaning of the Tokyo Trials was the declaration of peace of all countries in the world.

The Tokyo Trials also had a great impact in Japan. After learning of the trial results, the *Asahi Shimbun* published an editorial titled "The Worldwide Embodiment of the Determination of Peace" [Fig.2-17], in which it mentioned, "This verdict is of great significance to Japan and Japanese history, as well as to the world and world history, worth recording in the history." It "indirectly requires ordinary citizens who support the so-called 'national policy' and follow the defendant to conduct thorough introspection and liquidation, and also clearly stipulates that the country of Japan that our citizens will build in the future should be a country of peace. Furthermore, these requirements and regulations will always restrict the actions of Japanese nation, so that there will never be a time for trial any more in the future." It urged the Japanese people not to be victimized by the militarism, but to become a staunch defender of world peace.

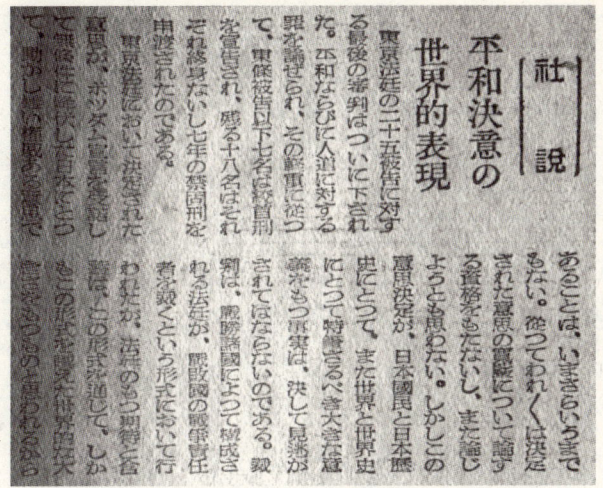

Fig.2-17 An Editorial "The Worldwide Embodiment of the Determination of Peace" Published in *Asahi Shimbun* (November 13, 1948)

The Nanjing Military Tribunal for the Trial of War Criminals was established in February 1946. As a city that suffered severe disaster in this war, the trial and disposal of war criminals not only reflected the "victory of the just", but also the "victory of the peace-loving". Peace without justice was not the true peace. This was a trial for peace, which declared to the world that justice would defeat evil. At the same time, it solemnly urged the world to stay away from war. The Chinese people should work tirelessly for the permanent peace of the world together with the people of the world including Japanese people to prevent the recurrence of historical tragedies.

Chapter 3
Calling for Peace

Historical memory is the core of all memories. Just as Anthony D. Smith said, "no memory, no identity; no identity, no nation." Historical memory is a reflection of national interests and political behavior, as well as adhesive of national unity. It often bears the mark of the times, so it is multi-faceted and constructive. It not only affects the real life of those who have witnessed it, but is also shared and continued by their descendants.

Fig.3-1 Nanjing City after the War

The city of Nanjing completely turned into "a panorama of hell" when the war ended. The originally thriving city turned into the scene of devastation, the population dropping sharply with few pedestrians on the dilapidated streets. Life production came to a standstill, and the market appeared chaotic. Nanjing, the former capital of China, lost its former prosperity. Compared with the burning, killing and looting by the Japanese army, environmental pollution, cultural plunder and the psychological trauma of the victims also wrought havoc on the city and its residents. The Japanese military tried to conceal the truth of history during the war, while their defeat also brought heavy disasters to the Japanese people.

The City Bearing Scars

The Devastated Homeland

After the war, about one-third of the buildings, from ordinary houses to cultural relics, were devastated in Nanjing. The business districts were destroyed most seriously. [Fig.3-2] The main commercial area, such as Confucius Temple, Xinjiekou, Taiping Road, and Zhonghua Road, all suffered enormous damage, all of which needed rebuilding. Many factories, shops, schools and dwelling houses were burned to a pile of ruins. The former prosperity disappeared without a trace.

Fig.3-2 **Destroyed Business District**

The water resource was severely polluted in the wartime. [Fig.3-3] Prior to the war, the daily drinking water was mainly fetched from ponds, Qinhuai River, wells, and the Yangtze River. On the eve of the Japanese invasion of Nanjing, some power supply and water supply were cut off in the city. During the massacre, corpses of the victims were scattered in ponds and lakes in and outside the city. A large number of corpses were thrown into the Yangtze River by the Japanese troops. The germs the corpses carried contaminated the drinking water, and the residents had to endure the torment of hunger and thirst. The pollution brought great inconvenience to their daily life after the war. A survivor recalled, "There has been no tap water supply since November. Drinking water is picked from the ponds. It is actually muddy water, but no one dares to go out to carry water, and they have to use it. We shared a basin of water to do washing every morning to save water. Later I learned that the yellow muddy water was soaked by the loyal and innocent soul."

Fig.3-3 Polluted Water Sources during the War

Fig.3-4 Seriously Damaged Zhongshan Gate

    The air was also badly polluted in Nanjing during the wartime, mainly because of the toxic chemicals produced by the Japanese artillery shells and the dense dust and smoke the burned buildings were giving off. After the Japanese army entered the city of Nanjing, they kept on with large-scale bombing and burning of buildings. The pungent smell was lingering in the air, and the burning matter drifted around with the wind. In addition, the bacteria produced by the corpse also filled in the air. In the cold winter, the corpses on the sides of the road gave off a rotting stench, hanging in the air everywhere, making it hard to breathe. The backlog of decomposing corpses caused great difficulty for the disposal. Some were not buried deep, some were exposed, and the bites of animals spread bacteria and diseases in every nook and cranny.

Fig.3-5 Nanjing City Wall Brick with Bullet Hole

The lush woods in places like Purple Mountain, Niushou Mountain, Fugui Mountain, became scorched, many trees were cut down, and flowers and greenery were trampled into the dust. A large collection of rare and valuable cultural relics were stolen from the Central Museum, which would be China's largest national museum that Nanjing was preparing to build. Books and documents stored in more than 70 places, such as the Academia Sinica and Jiangsu Provincial Library for Chinese Ancient Civilization, were also despoiled of. Furthermore, famous religious and cultural sites, like a number of temples and affiliated houses, such as Xianku Temple on Niushou Mountain, Youqi Temple, Flower Temple, Zudeng Temple on Zhenjiang Road, and Mosque in Xiaguan, were damaged or razed to the ground in the arson attack by the Japanese army. Scenic spots, like Zhongshan Gate [Fig.3-4], Purple Mountain, and Sun Yat-sen Mausoleum, were damaged and became scarred during the Japanese bombardment. Clear bullet marks can still be seen on the copper tripod of Sun Yat-sen Mausoleum. The image of a garden city and an ancient cultural capital no longer existed.

The wealth accumulated in the period of the modern industry was also robbed of or destroyed by the Japanese army during the catastrophe. According to statistics, the entire industry was damaged or destructed at a rate as high as 80%. These included the Yongli Power Plant, which was just completed and put into operation in 1937, and important equipment such as sulfuric acid tanks and water towers were all occupied by the Japanese or shipped back to Japan. Those factories that were too late to be transported were either completely destroyed or reduced to refugees' shelter. The war brought an abrupt halt to the modernization of Nanjing, and the "golden years" of the capital Nanjing was irreversible.

Fig.3-6 Queen Margaret II of Denmark (Third from Right) Unveiling the Statue of Sindberg

Nanjing Forever Sindberg Rose

Jiangnan Cement Plant, built in 1937, was the largest cement plant in China with the most advanced equipment and technology. Mr. Sun Yat-sen attached much importance of the plan to vigorously develop cement plants in his *Strategy for the Founding of the Country*, saying that "steel and cement are the foundation of modern architecture". In order to protect the equipment, the national asset, the National Government specially invited some foreign professionals to take care of it. Bernhard Arp Sindberg, who was in his 20s, was one of them, taking care of the imported Danish equipment. The war suspended the production of the factory, which was transformed into a "refugee zone". Sindberg had a giant Danish flag painted at the top of the factory building to prevent Japanese bombing. With his aid, this refugee camp protected more than 20,000 civilians in 106 days. He also documented the atrocities in the form of photos and letters. He was praised by the Chinese people for his "righteousness" and left a precious story in China-Denmark friendship.

To commemorate Sindberg's righteousness, a local yellow rose in his hometown, Aarhus, was named "Nanjing Forever Sindberg Rose" in 2004. In 2019, the Nanjing Municipal People's Government presented the Sindberg Statue to Aarhus, and Queen Margaret II of Denmark unveiled the bronze statue on the acceptance ceremony [Fig.3-6]. Standing on the city wall bricks of Nanjing, "Sindberg" with open arms symbolizes the good wishes of the Chinese and Danish peoples to build friendship and peace together.

Permanent Mental Trauma

The Nanjing massacre not only infringed on the personal and property safety of the Chinese people and Westerners, but left behind them memories of terror that psychologically troubled them. The spiritual havoc wrought by atrocities was beyond imagination. Once a violent act occurred, it was like a thorn deep in the heart. It was clearly known to be there and made people suffer, but it couldn't be got out. In the investigation of the victims, it was found that many of them were troubled by nightmares of violence. Some of them became abnormal in words and deeds. And as they grew older, this mental torture remained and went along with them, and even triggered a series of adverse reactions. The survivor Zhang Yuying suffered from schizophrenia. She had nightmares of the scene where her father was killed by the Japanese army. All massacre survivors might suffer from chronic anxiety, fear, depression, nightmares, irritability, neurological disorders, autism, hypochondria, and might even commit suicide due to loss of hope in the world. Similar psychiatric symptoms also appeared in the survivors of Nazi concentration camps, and it was adequate to verify that the atrocities had caused similar harm to humans.

Violent behavior occurred in the past, but it was likely to change a person's future life. This was well illustrated by Chang Zhiqiang, who survived from the massacre. He originally had a large family of 10 people, but he became an orphan when the atrocities happened. His parents and siblings all died in this man-made disaster. Chang Zhiqiang fainted due to excessive fright, only to get his life back and changed. Nevertheless, he was reluctant to mention this horrible experience, because he would fall into pain and could not get extricated once it was mentioned.

Foreigners who had chosen to remain in Nanjing during the war also experienced stress disorder after the war. When George Fitch left Nanjing to publicize the facts of the Nanjing massacre in the United States, he constantly suffered from amnesia and other symptoms. Although no problems were found in his brain through X-ray examination, he remarked, "The memories of terror that happened every day in Nanjing may be related to the nervous fatigue." There were those who suffered more seriously even giving up their will to live in the world. Ms. Vautrin, head of the refugee camp of Jinling Women's College of Arts and Sciences, blamed herself for not being able to save more refugees from the massacre. Finally, she committed suicide in the United States on May 14, 1941 to end the trauma from war. From this perspective, they not only were the compassionate rescuers in the war, but unfortunately became the victims of the atrocities.

Not only the person involved, but the historical researchers also bear the negative impact of this memory. When Zhang Chunru (Iris Chang) got closer to the darkness of the past, and bravely revealed the painful side of the history, the heavy truth brought her much mental pain and burden. Unbearable, she finally ended her young life by committing suicide. Unfortunately, her experience was not an isolated case, and the trauma left over by the atrocities is still going on from generation to generation.

Every survivor had a personal but similar traumatic memory. Victims who had experienced the atrocities of war in the world all had such a kind of feeling as spiritual destruction by violence. Terribly, it would not fade away as the body was healed. In most cases, it would only become more unforgettable, and might even lead to more conflicts and violence. Up to August 2022, there were only 50 odd survivors of the Nanjing Massacre, and the average age was close to 90 years old. As Bates put it, "Our intention of recalling the past, which is fraught with horror and crime, is not for revenge, but to seek truth and justice, and also to learn the lessons from the history." For every survivor, it is because they have experienced the cruelty of war that they don't want it to happen again. What they hope for is peace in the future.

"What I Hope for Is Peace"

In a family ritual by families of the deceased in 2016 for victims in Nanjing Massacre, Qiu Xiuying, an elderly woman, was crying when she recalled the scene of her mother being killed by the Japanese soldiers. "I was only 7 years old. The moment my mother and my brother were going out to dump waste, they were discovered by the Japanese soldiers. My mother was shot and killed on the spot, and my brother was taken away to do hard work for them. My father, witnessing all that happened, was about to rush out, but was held back in order to avoid unnecessary sacrifice, and to take care of the four children left." Qiu Xiuying told the reporters several times in choking, "I still hate the atrocities by the Japanese army in Nanjing that year, and now I have great-grandchildren, I often tell them what happened then. But what I hope for is peace. I hope there will be no more wars, and my children and grandchildren will no longer have to suffer wars and can grow up peacefully."

Fig.3-7 The Photo Wall of the Deceased Survivors of the Nanjing Massacre

历史的凝视 — 南京大屠杀幸存者照片墙
歴史を凝視 — 南京大虐殺生存者の写真パネル
The Gaze of History — Photo Wall of Survivors of the Nanjing Massacre

War Trauma beyond Borders

Japanese military atrocities caused unforgettable trauma to the Chinese people, while the war also brought spiritual and material torture to the Japanese soldiers and civilians.

In the summer of 1945, two atomic bombs were dropped down on Hiroshima and Nagasaki respectively by the United States, which accelerated the end of the war. On August 15, 1945, Emperor Hirohito of Japan announced the "Edict of the End of the War", the unconditional surrender of the Japanese Government through the broadcast. The war seemed to be over, but the trauma left over was far from over. Russell Brines, the first foreign journalist to enter Tokyo, was shocked by the miserable scene in front of him. "Everything was razed to the ground…" Data from the beginning of 1946 showed that Japan lost one third of its total property. The living standards in rural areas dropped to roughly 55% of the pre-war level, while those in urban areas dropped to 35%. 66 major cities across the country, including Hiroshima and Nagasaki, were severely bombed and destroyed, and at least about one third of the people became homeless. Apart from that, there were about 6.5 million Japanese citizens stranded in Asia, Siberia and the Pacific.

After the war, most of the Japanese expats and war criminals were repatriated. However, many of the wounded and disabled soldiers who returned to Japan could not be compensated accordingly and were unable to take care of their lives because of the collapse of Japan's economy after the war. In the end, they could only live on the streets, begging for life. They were physically and mentally disabled, and were filled with "the shame of defeat". The double discrimination made their situation even more miserable.

In the months after the surrender, notices for missing family members were posted in every nook and cranny of the streets in Japan. Nevertheless, wives, children, and parents were waiting for the return of their beloved ones day after day. Perhaps, what they were waiting for was a disabled person, but it was more hopeful than a cold corps or no news. More cruelly, for some returning expats, the urn, a special item, often appeared in their poor luggage. After many twists and turns they returned to their homeland from overseas, only to find their house in ruins and nowhere to go. Among them, many children lost their parents and siblings. Hunger and disease made these homeless itinerants more miserable. Parks, train stations, and shanty towns became new refuges for them. People who committed suicide and starved to death because of their inability to make a living could be seen everywhere. Begging and stealing became survival skills that the refugees need to master. After a long time passed, they were able to have the opportunity to receive education and change their destiny.

Similarly, the war left them with deeply spiritual devastation. In the memories of Japanese veterans, killings, on the one hand, made them crazy and thrilled, and on the other hand, plunged them into remorse and deep self-blame. According to the research conducted by Kuniko Muramoto at Ritsumeikan University, most of the Japanese soldiers who returned from the battlefield tended to be violent. The brutality of war and the suppression of the good made some of them no longer able to establish close relationships with their families. What was even more frightening was that if violence could not be effectively prevented, it would be passed on from generation to generation, especially for those who had to grow up in a violent environment. The spread of violence would strip off the good part of human nature and bear evil fruits.

There is no end to the trauma caused by the war. For most ordinary people, war has forever destroyed the life they were familiar with before. Dependence on violence and bigoted perception of self-interest will only make this tragedy more painful and unbearable. Once violence occurs, people will drift away from the goodness of the past. Therefore, the war and everything related to it have been extremely disgusting.

Reshaping the Memory

Acknowledging the authenticity of history is the basis for seeking common ground and preserving differences. Justice and truth is the prerequisite for reconciliation and forgiveness. Any party has the responsibility to ensure that the memory is preserved as truthfully as possible. At the same time, forgiveness must be premised on the belief that the source of hostility has been remedied and that individual and collective pain and hurt have been healed. However, the biggest problem is that if the perpetrator wants to beautify or even cover up the sinful facts of the past, how can he ask the victim for forgiveness?

Simon Wiesenthal told a story in his book *The Sunflower: On the Possibilities and Limits of Forgiveness* published in 1976. Before his death, a Nazi soldier who participated in the Holocaust confessed to Wiesenthal, a Jewish prisoner who had been held in a concentration camp, and asked for his forgiveness, but Wiesenthal chose to go away silently. This left the famous "Wiesenthal Question", namely, should the dying soldier be forgiven? Thirty years later, his book *The Sunflower* was published in a second edition, which included the responses by 44 experts to the book from around the world. As a result, almost everyone supported what Wiesenthal had done. Some people pointed out that "forgiveness is a virtue, but killing the innocent is an unforgivable sin"; others believed that "forgiveness is gentle apparently, but is very ruthless to the murdered".

"Forgiveness is a virtue, but it is never cheap." Forgiveness does not necessarily mean absolving sins or turning a blind eye to atrocities. One can offer forgiveness while pursuing justice, but the key is to learn to admit "the truth of the past". This is an interactive process, especially the perpetrators should actively respond to this history and reflect on war crimes. Only when all parties are convinced that the evils of the past will not come back, and that all is moving in the right direction, will they be freed from their painful confusion, recognize the reality and pin their hopes on the future.

Embroidering the Atrocities

The Japanese military once tried to conceal and embroider their act of invasion. They called their invasion of China and other countries in the Asia-Pacific region as helping with liberation from the colonial oppression of white people and the establishment of the "Greater East Asia Co-Prosperity Sphere". Due to their excessively strict control over news, it was difficult for both Chinese and Western media to get real information about Nanjing. Only Japanese military reporters were allowed to interview and report on the situation after the fall of Nanjing, and tried to spread the image of "a renewed Nanjing" to the outside world that the Chinese people warmly welcomed the Japanese troops with gratitude for their kindness. The fake news almost took up the space of Chinese newspapers, and it was also published in major Japanese newspapers, such as Japan's largest newspaper *Tokyo Asahi Shimbun*, *Asahi Pictorial*, *China Incident Pictorial*, etc., satisfying the needs of the Japanese authorities to stabilize the situation in Nanjing and suppress the international public opinion in wartime.

Almost all of the "propaganda photos" were taken in a specific situation by force or deceit, and the parties involved were mostly children, women, or vulnerable groups such as captured wounded Chinese soldiers, in order to create a harmonious atmosphere between the Chinese and Japanese military and civilians to beautify Japanese invasion of China. For example, a picture captioned "Chinese Wounded Soldier Receiving Treatment" published on the *Tokyo Asahi Shimbun* on December 22, 1937, showed that the Japanese military doctors and nurses in a hospital were diagnosing and treating the Chinese wounded soldiers. In response to these news, the *Hsin Shun Pao* created by the Japanese spy agency in Shanghai published on December 27 a piece of news that "the Japanese army set up three temporary hospitals in Nanjing to rescue Chinese wounded and sick soldiers". They cooked up that the Chinese soldiers who were rescued expressed their gratitude and even their willingness to fight for Japan.

However, some of the righteous Westerners who remained in Nanjing exposed the despicable tactics the Japanese soldiers were trying. After seeing the false report on the *Hsin Shun Pao*, John Magee wrote down in his diary that the (Japanese authorities) treatment of the wounded soldiers was done deliberately for propaganda, so as to conceal their prevailing unspeakable brutality. On January 6, 1938, Vautrin revealed in her diary how the Japanese reporters made fake news about refugees. She described that a few Japanese reporters came to take pictures and asked the women to smile as happily as they could in front of the lenses. However, no matter how they tried to conceal, the scared and horrified expressions on these Chinese faces were incompatible with the joyous faces of the Japanese soldiers, forming a sharp contrast.

On March 4, Georg Rosen, the German ambassador to China, also mentioned in a telegram that the Japanese soldiers had brought in beautiful colorful posters that depicted a "kind" soldier, cooker in hand and Chinese child on shoulder, whose poor loyal honest peasant parents were looking at this "good uncle" with gratitude, and that were filled with the warmth and happiness of the family. "Unfortunately, these colorful pictures are fabricated and they are like travel advertisements!" You could figure out that the fake news reports spread overseas, covering up the atrocities that were taking place in Nanjing, leaving some people in the world ignorant of the disaster that China was undergoing.

However, there were also some conscientious Japanese military reporters and writers. They expressed deep sympathy for the suffering of the Chinese people after witnessing the atrocities committed by the Japanese army. They also felt condemned and upset at fabricating false news, but seemed powerless in the face of the strict news control and regulations of Japanese military. Shinju Sato, a photographer of Japan's *Tokyo Niichi Shimbun* (now *Mainichi Shimbun*), witnessed the Japanese troops brutally killing a large number of captured Chinese soldiers in Nanjing Lizhi Society, but he did not film what was happening in front of him. Afterwards, he told his companion about what he had seen, and was asked why he hadn't taken those photos as a photographer. He answered that if he had taken those photos, he would have been killed, too.

At the time of Japan's surrender, the Japanese military ordered all news agencies to destroy all materials involved in the war, including those photos with the "Disapproval" stamp, hoping that this history would be concealed forever. However, there were some Japanese publishers who insisted on justice, such as Masao Takada, director of the photography department of the Mainichi Shimbun agency, who risked his life of transferring some "Disapproval" photos to the basement for preservation as valuable evidence for the world to understand the truth about that period of history. In 1977, the Mainichi Shimbun agency took out these old photos, reprinted them, edited and published them together with other historical images into the *Showa History of 100 Million People* (15 volumes) series of picture albums. In 1998, it was published separately as two volumes of *Disapproval Photo Album*, through which these old photos with a red stamp of "Disapproval" were released to the public. In the photo, the Japanese troops were marching and committing atrocities with weapons in a foreign country, and the lies woven before were self-defeating. The truth of history would not change although some pseudo-historical materials were still the "weapons" used by some Japanese to distort and deny the history of invasion.

War leaves a nation or country in a state of pain that can never be forgotten. The painful trauma takes a long time to heal, and it requires the joint efforts of every party involved. Among them, the Japanese side, as the perpetrator in this history, should have a more positive and correct attitude to recognize and remember this history. Only through the direct exposure to history can reflection, responsibility, and prosperity be achieved.

Photos Stamped with "Disapproval"

The Japanese authorities made strict regulations that each head office of news agency must develop four additional copies of the photo that was taken by military reporters and send them by air to the Ministry of the Army, the Ministry of the Navy, and the Intelligence Bureau of the Ministry of Foreign Affairs for approval. The three institutes kept one of them respectively, and the rest one was returned to the head office of each news agency. The photo was stamped differently to indicate their examination and handling opinions: the one stamped with "Approval" could be published in newspapers and periodicals; the one stamped with "Disapproval" was not allowed to publish in newspapers and magazines, or even be leaked. They wanted to create a good atmosphere of public opinion for the Japanese conquest, avoid the scenes of atrocities to trigger international and domestic protests and public outrage, and cause moral condemnation and international pressure on its follow-up actions.

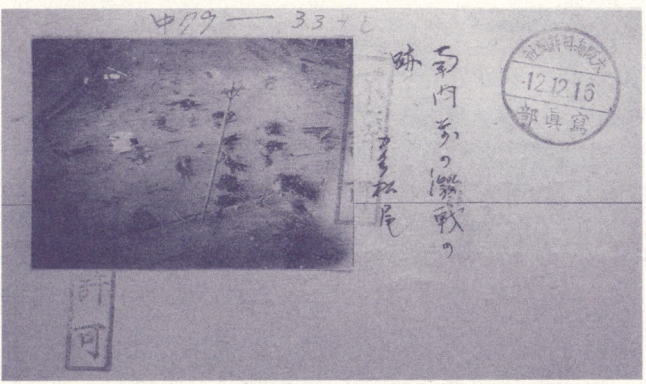

Fig.3-8 Photos Stamped with "Disapproval"

Arousal of Traumatic Memories

Although the war was over, it was imperative that the Chinese government and people should take seriously the issue of how to remember this history. Soon after the end of the war, the Nanjing authority held the "Memorial Meeting and Commemorative Ceremony for the Martyred Compatriots in the Capital Killed by the Enemy" in 1947 in order to mourn the victims of the Nanjing Massacre. Participants in the ceremony were representatives from more than 40 organizations, including the Nanjing Municipal Council, bureaus of the municipal government, the municipal party department, primary and secondary schools, and other organizations. *Central Daily News* and other newspapers reported on this event. The ceremony was hosted by Chen Yuguang, Chairman of the Nanjing Municipal Council, and all stood in silence in the mourning music. Shen Yi, mayor of Nanjing, emphasized that "this tragic day in history should be kept firmly in mind not only by Nanjing citizens, but by the entire Chinese nation…We must not forget this tragic fact". In order to get a better memorial effect, the Nanjing Municipal Council announced that the entertainment activities in the whole city that day should be halted for one day, but it had to be cancelled due to the deterioration of the economic situation. In 1951, Nanjing held a second memorial activity, but the publicity was not significantly strengthened.

In the 1960s, this historical memory was deeply influenced by the international settings of the Cold War and the complicated political situation in China. In 1972, Japanese Prime Minister Kakuei Tanaka visited China at the invitation of Premier Zhou Enlai. After friendly talks, the two countries signed the "Joint Statement between the Government of the People's Republic of China and the Government of Japan" in Beijing and established formal diplomatic relations. Due to the friendly atmosphere of "normalization of diplomatic relations between China and Japan", the Nanjing Massacre, as one of the major traumas of the war,

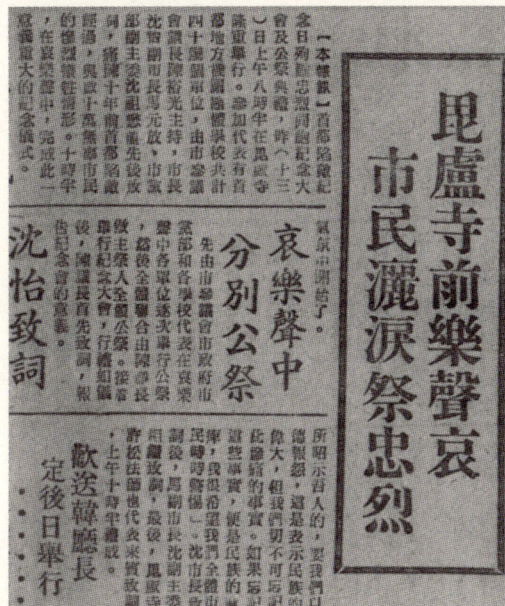

Fig.3-9 The Memorial Meeting and Commemorative Ceremony Reported in *Central Daily News* (December 14, 1947)

was rarely mentioned during that period. On the other hand, New China badly needed to maintain national self-esteem and enhance national self-confidence when she was in a critical period of construction and recovery. The negative impressions and emotions associated with the victims of violence unconsciously kept them isolated. Iris Chang wrote in her book, "The reason why the Nanjing Massacre did not penetrate into the consciousness of the people of the world like the Nazi holocaust of Jews or the Hiroshima atomic bomb was that the victims themselves remained silent."

After the promulgation of the "Full-Time Middle School History Syllabus (Draft)" in 1963, the information about the Nanjing Massacre gradually appeared in various curriculum standards or syllabuses, and became a fixed content in history textbooks, though in a relatively limited length. Meanwhile, the academic research on the history of the Nanjing Massacre was increasingly advancing, and enriched the content of the textbooks. The relevant pictures and historical materials increasingly improved, and the students' perception of that period of history was more delicate.

In 1982, "Japan's history textbook incident" alerted the Chinese people about this traumatic history. Japan's approval of the history textbooks written by nationalists for middle schools that distorted historical facts and glorified the invasion created dissatisfaction among East Asian countries and severely damaged the national sentiments of countries in the Asia-Pacific region that were victims of World War II. The Chinese government immediately lodged solemn representations with the Japanese side over the textbook issue. The *People's Daily* immediately issued a special comment titled "This Lesson Must Be Kept in Mind", in which it pointed out that if the Japanese side thought the incident had passed, and didn't want to throw a gloom over Japan's friendship with China and Southeast Asian countries… that's a big mistake and quite wrong. The Japanese militarism policy of invasion and expansion has brought serious disasters to the people of China and Southeast Asian countries, as well as to the Japanese people. The historical facts must be respected and must not be tampered with. It is only by doing this that the Japanese people and the people of China and Southeast Asian countries can "not forget the past, and guide the future", and that the friendship between Japan, and China and Southeast Asian countries can be consolidated and developed.

The great differences between the two countries on how to remember the war have left the wounds unhealed till this day. And in the course of the debate between the two sides, it will destroy the trust of both parties and make the road to wound healing more difficult, once there is a deviation from the truth, such as the intention to glorify the war crimes.

In order to maintain the historical truth and mourn the victims of the massacre, the citizens of Nanjing and people from all over the country appealed to the government to organize to build museums, revise history, and erect monuments. After China officially began to study, disseminate, and commemorate the history of the Nanjing Massacre in an organized and large-scale manner, the Chinese government was determined to build a Memorial Hall of the Victims in Nanjing Massacre by Japanese Invaders in Nanjing to show its strong response. Under the new historical background, this traumatic memory has been reshaped and interpreted, and it has also been given new connotations and missions.

Pursuit of the Historical Truth

Getting the historical truth is a prerequisite for a society that suffered from violent conflicts to heal the sequel of ethnic wound and to rebuild social trust and harmony. In particular, it is clarifying the truth, punishing the perpetrators according to the law, and rehabilitating the victims that are the foundation for cultivating a culture of peace and achieving peace-building. After the war, the history of the Nanjing Massacre was rarely mentioned for a while, and the social memory was evaded or distorted due to various subjective and objective reasons. However, at the end of the 20th century, the narrative and dissemination of the Nanjing Massacre attracted more and more attention from the government to civil organizations. Through various methods such as building memory venues, conducting academic research, and engaging artistic creation, the citizens of Nanjing explored and displayed historical scenes from the perspective of the victims, exposed the brutality of the war, disseminated the historical truth, provided justice for the victims, and promoted to convert the personal memory of the massacre into the collective memory.

Memorial Sites for Denouncing Violence

The Memorial Hall of the Victims in Nanjing Massacre by Japanese Invaders

At the end of 1983, the Nanjing Municipal People's Government, approved by the Jiangsu Provincial Committee of the Communist Party of China and the Jiangsu Provincial People's Government, began preparations for the building of a memorial hall, and established a leading group in charge of compiling the history, building the memorial hall and erecting a monument, with Zhang Yaohua, mayor of Nanjing city, working as the team leader. The memorial hall officially started to build on February 20, 1985 and was designed by Academician Qi Kang. In order to restore the authenticity of history, the site was specially selected at one of the mass graves of the Nanjing Massacre, with the theme of "life and death". The memorial hall covers an area of 22,000 square meters and a building area of 2,500 square meters. On August 15 of the same year, the Memorial Hall of the Victims in Nanjing Massacre by Japanese Invaders was completed and opened to the public.

In 2005, the Memorial Hall had a second-phase expansion in the charge of He Jingtang, a famous architecture academician. The expanded memorial hall covers a total area of 74,000 square meters. The site is still centered on the original victim site, and the halls with the three themes of war, killing, and peace, are lined up along the axis from east to west. The second-phase expansion project, the shape of which looks like a "peace ark" [Fig.3-10], highlights the dialectical thinking about peace and violence. In order to reduce the impact on the weight of the old hall, the new hall was built with part of the main body of the old hall buried underground, and the part above ground was like a "broken saber", which implies that justice defeats evil. At the same time, the whole memorial hall uses black and gray as the key colors, and creates a solemn atmosphere through various landscapes such as dead wood, sandstone, group carvings, and wall carvings.

Fig.3-10 A Panorama of the Memorial Hall of the Victims in Nanjing Massacre by Japanese Invaders

Walking into the memorial square, you can see an eye-catching and solemn cross monument [Fig.3-11], which is inscribed with the date of the Nanjing Massacre (December 13, 1937-January 1938). The granite wall by its side is inscribed with "300000 victims" in 11 languages. In designing the memorial monument, Academician Qi Kang used elements from the Christian "cross" for reference, which represents "salvation" in Christianity. For the victims of the Nanjing Massacre, the cross also symbolizes rest and a yearning for peace. Meanwhile, it warns people never to forget this history, and the perpetrators will eventually be punished and repent for their crimes.

The "Hall of Death" is reorganized on the basis of the original victim site. Within the memorial hall are three "mass graves" of the Nanjing Massacre covering an area of 170 square meters, displaying the remains of the victims found in 1984, 1998-1999 and 2006. The remains of the victims can clearly be seen through the transparent glass wall, where broken or deformed bones can obviously be seen from the remains, showing the characteristics of the corpse buried in a state of war, and the strong visual impact enhances the visitors' intuitive image of this traumatic history.

Fig.3-11 Cross Monument

The archives wall of the victims in the memorial hall displayed more than 12,000 boxes of archive materials about victims of the Nanjing Massacre. Open a file at hand and you can clearly see the personal information of the victim, such as his/her name, age and address before death, the time, location, and situation of being killed. Although this information is simple and scattered, it touches visitors' hearts with its authenticity. Then visitors enter the dark meditation hall, the candlelight on the water flickers, and the smooth granite wall reflects the candlelight to the distance, making people stop to meditate. A steel bridge crosses the surface of the water, and at its end is engraved, "Let the remains be buried, let the wronged souls rest in peace, turn the butcher knife into an alarm bell, engrave the names of the dead into a history book, let the children no longer fear, let the mother no longer cry, let the war stay away from mankind, and let peace prevail in the future."

Stepping out of the meditation hall, visitors walk through the tranquil promenade, and they can see a huge white memorial sculpture and a burning holy fire on a central altar outdoors, which calm down their grief and anger. Finally, they come to the end of the memorial hall—Peace Park, the bright and wide space in sharp contrast with the previous darkness and depression.

In the memorial hall, multimedia means, such as sound and light techniques, video, and scene setting, for example, civilian houses destroyed in the war, simulated battle scenes, voice and video interviews with the survivors, sculptures of Rabe, and so on, were utilized through the whole exhibition, which makes visitors feel as if they were in history, and enhances their sensory experience and emotional resonance. In addition, the themed large-scale sculptures and the paintings are also a major feature of the memorial hall. For example, the group sculptures of "compatriot victims" [Fig.3-12] outside the exhibition hall are all based on real historical figures, and they will bring visitors into that painful and heavy historical situation with strong visual impact.

Fig.3-12 Group Sculptures of "Compatriot Victims"

Nanjing Museum of the Site of Lijixiang Comfort Stations

Walking on the path along Lijixiang, it's hard to imagine that this unremarkable path used to be a most frightening place to the Nanjing women, because the Japanese military police lived in the houses on the other end of the road, where there were some common yellow buildings that were called a real "hell on earth". In November 2003, Park Young-Shim, an elderly Korean woman who was lured by the Japanese army to come to China as a "comfort woman" for three years, returned to Lijixiang of Nanjing when she was 81 years old, and she identified this heartbreaking site. Recalling her experience, she said, "My life was too miserable, and it's too much to write down in several books."

In 2015, an exhibition venue was built in the original comfort stations in Lijixiang of Nanjing. It is the first memorial site in mainland China with the theme of "comfort women", and it is also a branch of the Memorial Hall of the Victims in Nanjing Massacre by Japanese Invaders. At the entrance to the exhibition venue, there is a bronze statue based on Park Young-Shim [Fig.3-13], the Korean "comfort woman". The statue consists of three "comfort women", one kneeling with loose hair, one holding her pregnant belly, touching and comforting the kneeling woman, and the other holding one of them to cover her face and crying. On the wall opposite to their back, there are over a dozen huge "teardrops", reflecting the sadness and helplessness of these "comfort women". On the facade of another building, there are black and white portraits of 70 survivors of the "comfort women", whose faces express the humiliation and pain left by the atrocities. Under the photo wall, a patch of land has been left, which is "moist all year round", symbolizing that the tears of the victims will never dry up.

With the theme of "tears", the exhibition of more than 1,600 cultural relics and nearly 700 photos illustrate the serious harm caused by Japanese invaders to "comfort women" in China and other countries and regions. Part of the exhibition areas restores the historical scenes of the comfort station, including the daily necessities and the cell of the "comfort women", and uses videos, relief sculptures, objects, photos and other methods to enhance the sense impression and interaction of the visitors. The Japanese military comfort stations scattered almost all over the occupied areas of southern China. In Shanghai alone, there were at least 160 comfort stations that could be identified. During the war, some women from Asian countries and regions, such as the Philippines, Myanmar, the Korean Peninsula and the Malay Peninsula, were also victims of the "comfort women" system. Every exhibit in the memorial venue is a painful memory of the female victims. However, the issue of "comfort women" has not yet been fully recognized by the international community. In June 2014, the Chinese government began to prepare files on the "comfort women" to apply for the "Memory of the World", and this work is still ongoing. The purpose is not to perpetuate the hatred, but to let people all over the world understand this

Fig.3-13 The Bronze Statue of "Comfort Women" in Front of the Former Site of Lijixiang Comfort Stations

system of "comfort women" was a serious violation of human nature, and learn from it, so that history will not repeat itself. China will not forget this painful experience, nor will the world.

John Rabe and International Safety Zone Memorial Hall

There is a tranquil courtyard at No.1 Xiaofenqiao, Guangzhou Road of Nanjing. Through a slightly narrow front door, a hidden two-storied Western-style villa comes to your eyes, where a German businessman, John Rabe, "Good Man of Nanjing" called by later generations, once lived.

In 1997, Nanjing University began to protect Rabe's former residence and planned to build it into a memorial venue with the support of the Nanjing Municipal People's Government. In December 2005, Nanjing University and the German Consulate General in Shanghai, Siemens (China) Co Ltd, Jiangsu Bosch-Siemens Home Appliance Sales Company and other parties signed agreements on Sino-German joint construction of the "John Rabe and International Safety Zone Memorial Hall" and "Rabe Research and Exchange Center for Peace and Conflict Resolution". The opening ceremony was held on October 31, 2006.

Thousands of historical materials from all over the country, the archives of the German Ministry of Foreign Affairs and Rabe's relatives were collected for the memorial hall, and finally over 300 pictures, 50 plus physical objects and 4 video recordings were publicly displayed. There is also a small shelter in the corner of the yard, which was used to protect refugees during the air raid. The memorial hall has received more than 200,000 visitors from China and abroad since its establishment over a decade ago, and was selected as the "International Cyber Peace Museum" in 2010. It has organized and participated in many cultural exchange activities for years, and has established an international volunteer service team to spread Rabe's deeds and translate related historical materials to the visitors. Today, it has become a messenger of peace exchanges, and it also carries the friendship between the Chinese and German people.

Nanjing Non-Governmental Museum of War of Resistance against Japanese Aggression

In a small building on Andemen Street, Yuhua District of Nanjing, there is a privately-run museum with the theme of the War of Resistance against Japanese Aggression. Wu Xianbin, the curator, has successively invested over 10 million yuan to gather related relics at various locations throughout the country, and has collected oral history by visiting veterans and Nanjing Massacre survivors since 2006. There are more than 5,900 pieces of cultural relics, including historical photos, physical objects, newspapers and magazines, writings, artworks, and various war medals related to the Nanjing Massacre, as well as valuable historical data, such as video recording of the war veterans, in the museum. The fourth floor is a reference room, where there are more than 40,000 books on the Chinese People's War of Resistance against Japanese Aggression, among which there are more than 2,000 unique copy on this history. The museum guarantees 300 days open to the public a year, and it receives more than 50,000 visitors each year, which is a quite influential private museum in Nanjing.

"The national memory can only be formed by integrating the official memory with the folk memory." The exhibits here are not too bloody, but just real historical figures and events. On the third floor of the museum, the most impressive thing is the message wall of the handprints left by the veterans who had fought in the War of Resistance against Japanese Aggression [Fig.3-14]. There are more than 2,000 red "hand models" and signatures of them hanging on it. It took 8 years to visit the veterans and get 300,000-minute oral data on that history. The collectors are racing against time. As time goes by, these veterans will eventually pass away, but their stories will remain in the museum forever for visitors to listen to and think about, so their heroic spirit will live on.

Fig.3-14 A Handprint Message Wall of the Veterans Involved in the War of Resistance against Japanese Aggression

A line of small characters, "A place to find heroes", can be seen at the entrance of the museum. For an auspicious nation, it can't go on without heroes. These heroes were all common people, both ordinary and extraordinary. When their country was invaded and the nation was in grave peril, they risked their lives to guard peace and defend their hometown without hesitation. Their stories give us a deeper understanding of the essence of patriotism and a necessity to pay a tribute to those revolutionary martyrs. There are two concise sentences on the museum emblem, "NO WAR", and "Save the nation together from the crisis". Every piece of cultural relics and the faces that truly existed demonstrate the heroic spirit of winning victory for justice and peace. Even in an era of peace today, we still need this kind of heroic sentiment. It teaches us to be an awe-inspiring, fearless, loyal and daring person, and encourages us to forge ahead on the road of chasing dreams and peace.

Nanjing Anti-Japanese Aviation Martyrs Memorial Hall

After the war broke out, the pilots of the Chinese Air Force, who had only received short-term learning and training, resolutely flew to the blue sky and desperately fought with the Japanese against their bombardment. A large number of elites spilled their blood in the blue sky, and the aircrafts were almost completely damaged. During the war, more than 6,000 pilots and ground crews of the Chinese Air Force sacrificed or died at their posts, and 7,897 air force officers and soldiers were injured or disabled. In time of crisis, governments, organizations and individuals in many countries extended a helping hand. Pilots, ground crews, and other professionals from the Soviet Union, the United States, and South Korea, regardless of their personal safety, came to the Chinese battlefield, fought side by side with the Chinese army, and transported supplies for the fronts.

When the war was over, the government specially built a cemetery to commemorate these international aviation martyrs who had devoted their lives heroically to the war. In September 1995, the "Monument to the Aviator Martyrs in the War of Resistance against Japanese Aggression" [Fig.3-15] was built above the cemetery. In 2008, the Nanjing Municipal People's Government set up the "Nanjing Anti-Japanese Aviation Martyrs Memorial Hall" at the northern foot of Purple Mountain. It is the first and only one themed museum that integrates cemetery, monument and memorial hall in China. The heroic deeds of the Chinese air force and the international aid air force are fully displayed through the exhibitions on historical materials, sculptures, fighter aircraft models, historical images and other forms.

Fig.3-15 Monument to the Aviator Martyrs in the War of Resistance against Japanese Aggression

Upholding Justice like a Western Cowboy

Robert Short, a native of Washington State, was hired by the Boeing Aircraft Company to come to China as a jet test pilot and instructor. In 1932, when the Battle of Songhu broke out, Robert Short, who arrived in Shanghai, witnessed the indiscriminate bombardment of Japanese aircrafts in China, killing and wounding many innocent civilians. Indignant, he wrote in his diary that he hoped to be like a Western Cowboy, flying a fighter plane to mete out the bombers.

On February 20, 1932, Robert Short flew a Boeing 218 fighter jet to Nanjing and encountered three bombers taking off from the Japanese "Kaga" aircraft carrier. The battle was fierce and lasted for nearly 30 minutes, and he got one of them injured.

On February 22, Robert Short flew a jet to patrol the sky over Suzhou and suddenly discovered that six Japanese fighter jets were shooting and bombing the Chinese civilians. He resolutely rushed into the blue sky to protect them disregarding his personal safety. However, his jet was hit by the Japanese air force due to his fighting alone, and he died when he was only 27 years old.

The Chinese soldiers and civilians under his protection were in deep sorrow after hearing his death. The Chinese government posthumously awarded him captain of the air force and invited Short's family from thousands of miles away to join in the grand funeral ceremony held for him. Tens of thousands of Chinese people spontaneously went to see off this air-force hero for the last time. Today, this renowned martyr's name was engraved on the Monument to the Aviator Martyrs in the War of Resistance against Japanese Aggression, and the Nanjing Aviation Cemetery retains his cenotaph for mourning and commemoration.

There are 30 black subordinate steles in the cemetery, engraved with the names of 3,306 Chinese and foreign aviation martyrs (882 Chinese, 236 Soviet soldiers, 2,186 Americans, and 2 South Koreans), for people to pay a tribute to. On each side of the stele, the name, position or military rank, place of origin, date of birth and death of each martyr are neatly engraved, including frontline combatants, some ground staff and pilot students. The Aviation Martyrs' Cemetery has unfortunately been damaged repeatedly in history, and it has received financial support from the government and donations from patriots in China and abroad during the long restoration process. The designer of the memorial hall and the monument is Mr. Meng Fanhua from Beijing, who put the collaborative spirit of the international air force into his design. In front of the monument, there are two pairs of small sculptures. One shows Chinese and Soviet pilots, named "Setoff", and the other, in the shape of two banners of victory, is Chinese and American pilots, called "Triumph". [Fig.3-16] Although the pilots came from different countries, they all had a common wish, that is, to defend peace when the aircraft was fighting in the sky.

There have been 40 memorial places (martyrs' tombs) in Nanjing to mourn the martyrs who died in the War of Resistance against Japanese Aggression. The "Memorial Sites of Martyrs in the War of Resistance against Japanese Aggression" are divided into four categories: cemetery, comprehensive cemetery, single tomb, and monument. At present, there were six venues listed in the categories of the memorial facilities and sites at the national level in Nanjing: The Memorial Hall of the Victims in Nanjing Massacre by Japanese Invaders, Nanjing Anti-Japanese Aviation Martyrs Memorial Hall, the Former Venue of the Ceremony for Japan's Surrender in China Theater, Rabe's Former Residence, the Former Site of the Lijixiang Comfort Stations of the Japanese Invaders and the Yuntai Mountain Anti-Japanese Martyrs Cemetery. The venues and memorial halls, as a powerful platform for spreading history and as memory carriers of historical events, are of great significance to the shaping and dissemination of historical memories and patriotism

Fig.3-16 Two Figure Sculptures in Front of the Monument—"Setoff" and "Triumph"

education. However, memorial venues' role as a public educational institution cannot be limited to revealing past atrocities and victims, but also working towards bridging the gap left by conflict. Their utility of building a culture of peace remains to be further explored.

Historical Research Focusing on the Truth

For many years, historical research has always been a critical factor to support and guarantee the understanding of the Nanjing Massacre, and it also highly reflects the trend of this collective memory. In 1960, a detailed investigation and research on the Nanjing Massacre was conducted by Professor Gao Xingzu of Nanjing University, with a group of students who were majoring the Japanese history in the History Department of Nanjing University. A book of their achievements, *The Massacre of the Japanese Imperialists in Nanjing*, came out in 1962 only for university internal teaching. It was not published until 1979, but circulated only inside Nanjing University. This book was the first comprehensive narrative of that period of history in China. The author, Gao Xingzu, born in 1928, underwent the cruelty of the Japanese War of Aggression against China; especially his family members lost their precious lives in the war. Therefore, he hoped that more people could know and face this disaster, and never forget the tens of thousands of victims in the war. However, the massacre research was not considered a hot issue at that time, so his work did not receive much attention, and it took a lot of trouble to find a publishing house that was willing to publish his research result. But soon after, the research on the history of the Nanjing Massacre heated up in China due to the "Japan's history textbook incident" and the situational changes in China and the world. In 1985, Gao Xingzu's book of *Atrocities of the Japanese Invaders in China: The Nanjing Massacre* was published, which was the first monograph to systematically introduce the Nanjing Massacre in China. This booklet fully revealed the whole story of the Nanjing Massacre for the first time, and it was translated into Japanese and published in Japan later.

Thereafter, scholars in China have published works one after another to reveal the historical truth, and the research on the history of the Nanjing Massacre has gradually been on the right track. After years of painstaking efforts, a group of scholars ranging from old, middle-aged to young have come into being in the field of research on the history of the Nanjing Massacre, forming a relatively stable professional research team, and gaining a certain influence in academic circles in China and abroad. With expansion of the research team and content, popular readers such as novels, reportage, and picture books have gradually been added besides the academic monographs, to spread historical facts in multiple languages, to different age groups and from various aspects. This historical memory has increasingly imprinted in the minds of Chinese people through hundreds of research writings, the translation from various languages, the recordings of the survivors' experience, and the constantly discovered historical facts.

In 2011, *The Collection of Historical Materials on the Nanjing Massacre* was published, which is currently the most informative collection of historical materials on the Nanjing Massacre. This series has 78 volumes, more than 40 million characters, and it took ten years to complete. The compilers collected documents and oral materials from archives, historical archives, research institutes and other institutions in the United States, the United Kingdom, Germany, Japan and other countries, and finally sorted them out into volumes. In addition, China has also introduced some research results of Japanese scholars and translated them into Chinese. For example, Japanese scholar Hora Tomio's *Nanjing Massacre* (1987), Michio Tsuda's *Nanjing Massacre and the Mental Structure of the Japanese* (1995), and *A Hundred Days inside the Nanjing Refugee Zone* (2005) by Kasahara Tokushi, etc. These works express the justice of Japanese progressive scholars on safeguarding historical truth and condemning the violence of war, and enhance the international understanding of massacre research.

In 2021, a book, *Japanese Atrocities in Nanjing: The Nanjing Massacre and Post-Massacre Social Conditions Recorded in German Diplomatic Documents*, was published by co-author of the Memorial Hall of the Victims in Nanjing Massacre by Japanese Invaders in China and Shuping Lu, a Chinese professor at the University of Nebraska in the United States. This book includes the telegrams, letters, reports and other diplomatic documents sent by German diplomatic officials in Nanjing to the Foreign Office in Berlin and the German Ambassador in China after the Nanjing Massacre, and it is of great historical value.

Furthermore, international academia, especially overseas Chinese scholars, is paying more and more attention to that period of history. The most famous one at the early days was Iris Chang (with her Chinese name Zhang Chunru), American-Chinese female writer, who wrote *The Rape of Nanking: The Forgotten Holocaust of World War II*.

When Chang was a little girl, she heard of the Nanjing Massacre from her parents. They grew up in China during World War II and went into exile after the war, so they would never forget the war atrocities of the Nanjing Massacre. When they occasionally talked about the holocaust, Chang could not understand that much, but she was curious about it. She looked it up (in her school library), and found it difficult to get specific details and evidence about the massacre. When she became a professional writer twenty years later, she came across old photos about the Japanese atrocities in Nanjing, and this dust-sealed memory entered her life again. A question arose spontaneously, why Westerners knew much about the crimes of the German Nazis, but had little knowledge of the atrocities of the Japanese army in China, and this made Iris Chang shocked and furious. After that, she decided to devote herself to this research, to explore the truth of that period of history and reveal it to the public, hoping to keep this important part of historical memory all over the world.

Documents of Nanjing Massacre Included in UNESCO Memory of the World International Register

In 2015, eight years of meticulous preparation witnessed the documents of Nanjing Massacre officially taken in UNESCO Memory of the World International Register.[Fig.3-17] The Memory of the World International Register, as an extension of the World Cultural Heritage Project (including cultural heritage, natural heritage, cultural-and-natural heritage), is a documentary protection project initiated by UNESCO in 1992, with the purpose of rescuing the aging, damaged, and disappearing documents around the world in an effort to preserve human memory intact through international cooperation and technological means. According to UNESCO's official website, the documents of Nanjing Massacre submitted by China fall into three categories, the files of the massacre of Chinese soldiers and civilians during the occupation of Nanjing by the Japanese invaders from 1937 to 1938; archives of post-war investigations and trials of Japanese war criminals from 1945 to 1947; and documents provided by the Judiciary of the People's Republic of China from 1952 to 1956. These materials fully illustrate that the Nanjing Massacre is an undeniable historical fact and a historical memory that cannot be forgotten.

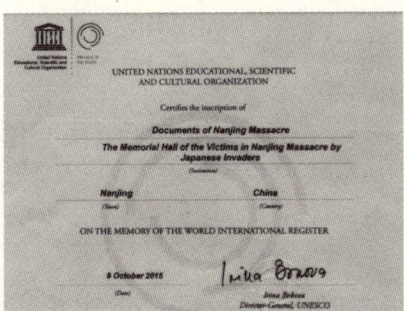

Fig.3-17 Documents of Nanjing Massacre Were Included in the Memory of the World International Register (2015)

It took Chang nearly three years to make enquiries from the survivors worldwide, collect a large amount of source materials in Chinese, Japanese, German and English, as well as original materials of diaries, notes, letters, and government reports that had never been published. While reading and collecting these historical data, Chang often shed tears and trembled with anger. In a later book, she wrote, although I heard many things about the Nanjing Massacre when I was a child, I was never ready to see these photos; at this extremely painful moment, I was aware that not only life was fragile, but human experience itself was also frail.

Chang visited Nanjing in 1995 and interviewed the survivors of the massacre and documented their stories. Many of these survivors were hopeless all their life for fair apology and compensation from the perpetrators. She realized that the pain she read in lines did exist in real life, and it was even more unacceptable and shocking; this city, this country, suffered too much of pain, but it was rarely known. This made Chang determined to save those who were forgotten and speak for those who could no longer speak.

In 1997, the book was finally published in the United States and immediately caused a sensation in the West. It was reprinted 15 times and was hailed as "the first book in English to comprehensively study the Nanjing Massacre". Chang was a hero, for she bravely presented that period of history to the Westerners. However, she was psychologically depressed due to long-term writing on such dark subjects. In 2004, she committed suicide in her car and ended her young life at the age of only 36.

Iris Chang: *The Rape of Nanking* (Excerpt)

This book provides only the barest summary of the cruel and barbaric acts committed by the Japanese in the city, for its aim is not to establish a quantitative record to qualify the event as one of the great evil deeds of history, but to understand the event so that lessons can be learned and warnings sounded. Differences in degree, however, often reflect differences in kind, and so a few statistics must be used to give the reader an idea of the scale of the massacre that took place sixty years ago in a city named Nanking.

One historian has estimated that if the dead from Nanking were to link hands, they would stretch from Nanking to the city of Hangchow, spanning a distance of some two hundred miles. Their blood would weigh twelve hundred tons, and their bodies would fill twenty-five hundred railroad cars. Stacked on top of each other, these bodies would reach the height of a seventy-four-story building.

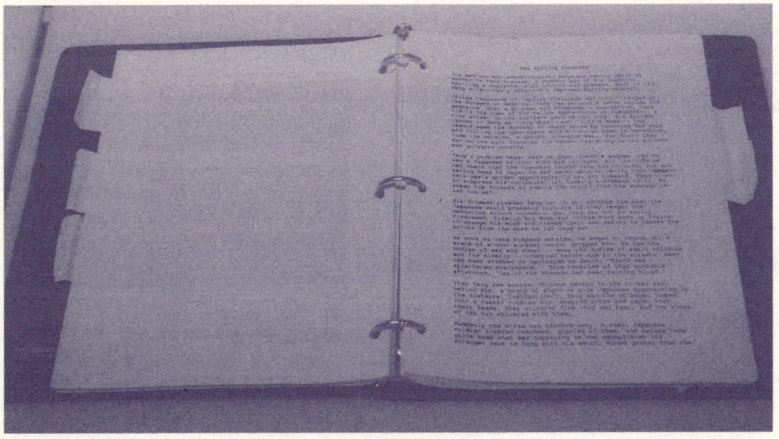

Fig.3-18 The English Manuscript of Iris Chang's *The Rape of Nanking*

At the same time, books from perspectives of the third party, such as *Rabe's Diary*, *Vautrin's Diary*, *Collections of Testimonies of Foreigners in Nanjing Massacre by Japanese Invaders*, *Nanjing Massacre—Reports by British and American Witnesses*, *Nanjing Massacre (1937-1938) in the Eyes of American Missionaries*, and *The Diary of Azuma Shiro* from the perspective of the perpetrators have also been successively translated and published in China.

The Diary of Azuma Shiro is one of the most special ones because the author was a Japanese infantryman in the Japanese War of Aggression against China. He documented what he had seen and heard during the war, leaving a five-volume wartime diary with 370,000 characters, depicting the inner world of a war perpetrator.

After Japan was defeated, Azuma Shiro received leniency from the Chinese government, was repatriated safely to his country and lived an ordinary life there. He felt remorseful whenever he thought of the atrocities he had committed against the Chinese. However, he could not defy the army's orders, nor could he change the history as an ordinary soldier. Therefore, at the 1987 Peace Exhibition in Kyoto, Japan, Azuma Shiro decided to release his wartime diaries, which included materials recording the scenes of the Nanjing Massacre, to express his deep reflection on the brutality of the Japanese War of Aggression against China. In December of the same year, Azuma Shiro submitted some excerpts from his diaries to the Aoki Shoten Publishing Company for publication, which evoked a stir in Japan and abroad, but was attacked by Japanese right-wing forces. In 1993, Japanese right-wingers even sued Azuma Shiro, Aoki Shoten Publishing Company, and the editor of the book, Masaki Shimozato, on the grounds of "fabricated stories" and "damaged reputation".

In spite of all the difficulties, Azuma Shiro never abandoned his pursuit of justice. In addition to publishing a diary, he also came to China seven times successively to apologize and repent in different ways. When he came to Nanjing for the fourth time, he donated his wartime diaries, medals and military flags to the Memorial Hall of the Victims in Nanjing Massacre by Japanese Invaders. He then commissioned the memorial hall to authorize Jiangsu Education Publishing House to publish his book of *The Diary of Azuma Shiro* in Chinese. Azuma Shiro, who was involved in the war, believes that telling the truth about the victims is the basis for reflection, which is an inescapable obligation and responsibility for those participating in the war.

In terms of academic exchanges, various thematic seminars have been organized in China, and meanwhile, there is a trend of international academic exchanges and multilateral cooperation among academic institutions, as research on the history of the Nanjing Massacre goes further. For example, the "International Symposium on History of Nanjing Massacre" sponsored by the Association for History Research on Nanjing Massacre by Japanese Invaders and other organizations was held in Nanjing in 1997, and only over 10 Japanese and American scholars attended the meeting. On December 13, 2011, the "International Symposium on 1937 in Historical Memory" was organized and held by the Memorial Hall of the Victims in Nanjing Massacre by Japanese Invaders, and more than 60 people including scholars and guests from countries such as China, the United States, Portugal, the Czech Republic, Greece, India, Nepal, South Korea, and related personnel from the memorial hall attended the meeting. At the seminar, a representative from the Greek World Peace Council said in his speech that the Greek people expressed admiration for the Chinese soldiers and civilians for their heroic resistance against Japanese imperialist invaders. The Indian representative remarked that the massacre atrocities committed by the Japanese invaders in Nanjing in 1937 were incredible and should be remembered by the whole world. In contrast, there are relatively fewer overseas academic activities on Nanjing Massacre history.

A few international academic seminars on the issue of the Nanjing Massacre were held in Japan, the United States and other countries, but the exposure and influence were relatively limited.

> ### "Nanjing Massacre Information Hotline" in Japan
>
> The Remembrance Society (Meishinkai), a Japanese civilian group, is dedicated to exploring the historical truth of the Nanjing Massacre, and has been engaged in investigation and research on the relevant historical facts for many years. In the past 30 years, the president of the society Matsuoka Tamaki has interviewed hundreds of war witnesses and victims, probed into the truth, published their testimonies into books and made them into films, to reveal this history to the world. Matsuoka Tamaki was a primary school teacher. When she taught students history, she discovered that Japanese textbooks distorted and played down the history of invasion of China. In her view, the role of education should be played in cultivating children's impartiality and telling them the truth of history. In order to explore the historical truth, the "Nanjing Massacre Information Hotline" was set up in 1997 in 6 cities including Tokyo, Nagoya, Osaka, and Hiroshima by the Japanese Remembrance Society and China-Japan Friendship Promotion Association, to collect perpetrators' testimony and other materials from Japanese veterans who had participated in the Japanese War of Aggression against China. The members of the investigation team also visited over 200 Japanese veterans who had participated in the Nanjing Massacre, and collected testimonies from victims in Nanjing on many occasions, shooting a lot of precious video clips. These conscientious Japanese people are not afraid of hardships and spontaneously collect historical data of war to maintain the truth of history. They believe that without understanding the tribulation of war, people won't cherish the preciousness of peace.

Arts on the Traumatic Memory

As for popular literature, novelists wrote about the distress of "national subjugation and family destruction" under the narrative of "family and nation" in that period, expressing the nationalists' shouts and worries about their nation and the people. During the War of Resistance against Japanese Aggression, there were literary works such as Huang Liugu's *Nominally Adoptive Mother*, Ah Long's *Nanjing Blood Sacrifice*, Zhang Henshui's *Eastward Flows the Great River*, and *Moment in Beijing* and *The Sound of Crane* written by Lin Yutang, who lived overseas, and other literary works. Zhang Henshui's *Eastward Flows the Great River* was created in 1939, based on historical facts such as the Nanjing defense war, the Nanjing Massacre, and the fall of Nanjing. It narrates a young soldier's patriotism and love for his children during the war. The author's words between the lines denounce the disasters caused by the war to the people, and reveal this unforgettable national tragedy. After the founding of New China in 1949, the works of writers such as Tang Ren, Li Gui, Li Erzhong, Wang Huo, Ge Liang, and Ha Jin, have all related to the historical memory of the Nanjing Massacre.

Among the female writers, the most representative one is the American-Chinese writer, Yan Geling, who created *Thirteen Flowers of Nanjing*. Although the characters in this novella are "fictional", its historical background is true. It mainly tells the story of thirteen brothel women who sacrificed their lives to save the female college students when Nanjing was occupied. The plot is interspersed with the Japanese troops' shooting Chinese soldiers and the massacre on the beach of the Yangtze River. Each and every typical scene, such as piles of corpses, brave national army, brutal enemies, dedicated prostitutes, international friendship and assistance, vividly presents the history before the readers' eyes. The techniques of inverted character setting and meticulous description of violence arouse readers' emotional resonance, awaken and touch people, and reflect on the good and evil of human nature.

In recent years, related topics have also attracted the attention of foreign writers. *The Storm Flower: Nanjing 1937* is a fictional novel written by Dave Davies, an English writer, based on the history of the Nanjing Massacre. Davies' grandfather was a veteran of World War II, from whom he heard the story of the Nanjing Massacre when he was a boy. In 2012, he visited the Memorial Hall of the Victims in Nanjing Massacre by Japanese Invaders, and was greatly touched by the tragic war and the testimonies of the survivors, which inspired him to write a book on this subject. Subsequently, he began to collect relevant information and looked into the history of that period. He found that what happened in China was too far away, compared to the European enemies that the British faced in World War II. Westerners knew very little about that period of history, and even had some misunderstandings of it, so he decided to write about the Nanjing Massacre. He said, "One of my purposes in publishing this novel in English and Chinese is to bring that history to Western readers. I hope that there will be one more voice to tell that history. Although voice of one person will not change everything, the history will gradually be remembered by more people if it is widely read."

Films convey this traumatic memory in a more intuitive and rapid way. In 1987, *Massacre in Nanjing* produced by Fujian Film Studio and Nanjing Film Studio was the first film in China on the theme of the Nanjing Massacre. The film director, Luo Guanqun, came to Nanjing for work in 1958, but he knew little about the history of the Nanjing Massacre. It wasn't until the early 1980s that he happened to read the "Japan's history textbook incident" in the newspaper, and he gradually learned the truth about the holocaust. Then, he accompanied his father to visit the newly-completed Memorial Hall of the Victims in Nanjing Massacre by Japanese Invaders, which also encouraged him to put it on the screen. The clues of the film came from 16 real photos found by Luo Guanqun in the Second Historical Archives of China. They were taken by the Japanese soldiers during the Nanjing Massacre. When the Japanese soldiers developed these photos in a photo studio in Nanjing, Luo Jin, an apprentice in the photo studio, secretly developed additional copies and kept them secretly. Luo Jin's story became the prototype of the *Massacre in Nanjing* film. In the first month of its premiere in Nanjing, 1.4 million people watched it. It was the first attempt on the subject of the Nanjing Massacre and won the Feature Film Award at the 1991 Tokyo International Peace Film Festival. Since then, the films released include *Black Sun: The Nanjing Massacre* (1995), *Don't Cry, Nanking* (1995), *Nanjing! Nanjing! (City of Life and Death,* 2009), and *John Rabe* (2009), a biographical film of the Nanjing Massacre, and *Iris Chang: The Rape of Nanking* (2008), a documentary film, and so on. The novella *Thirteen Flowers of Nanjing* mentioned above was also put on the big screen by Zhang Yimou in 2011 and became a popular Chinese movie of the year. These films preserve and disseminate historical memories through lenses, vividly presenting the bloody evidence of the Nanjing Massacre and the individual images in it. While allowing the audience to perceive the brutality of the war, these films also imprint people on their mind with more fear of that period of history and consolidate people's memory on the tribulation of Nanjing residents at that time.

The film of *Nanjing! Nanjing!* tells the nobodies involved in the war by using simple black and white pictures from the perspective of a Japanese soldier and an ordinary Chinese soldier. In contrast, this film has reduced the horrible and bloody war scenes, and does not directly judge the good and the evil in the war. The director hopes that the audience can take the initiative to think about the relationship between people in the war and the relationship between people and war. In the same year of 2009, another film *John Rabe* was adapted from the real story of John Rabe, and was a Sino-French-German co-production film directed by German director Flore Gallenberg. This film portrays the story of a group of foreign friends headed by Mr. Rabe establishing a safety zone in Nanjing to protect Chinese refugees. It is called the Chinese version of *Schindler's List*.

Painting is also one of the major ways to present historical memory, and it also has unique advantages in expressing and dissemination of the memory. The huge oil painting *Nanjing Massacre: Butchery, Surviving and Buddhism* by Li Zijian, a famous Chinese painter, is the brainchild of his continuous work for more than 80 days and nights with reference to a large number of historical photos and texts. He successively produced three paintings, and they are respectively displayed at the Memorial Hall of the Victims in Nanjing Massacre by Japanese Invaders, the Central Hall of the National Museum of China, and the Li Zijian Art Museum in Changsha.

The whole painting, 3.2 meters wide and 2.1 meters high, is composed of a triptych of "Butchery", "Surviving" and "Buddhism". The main body of the picture is a mountain of corps. On the left are two Japanese officers standing arrogantly, one wiping the bayonet in his hands, and under their feet are the heads of the killed, and it is named "Butchery". On the right is a monk who bows in silence, sadly dealing with the dead body of an old man, which is called "Buddhism". At the top of the corps mountain is a baby sitting on its mother's body and crying with its head up, and this is named with "Surviving". It implies the sadness of the Chinese nation, and also symbolizes its future and hope. The whole oil painting uses cool gray and dark red to create a solemn and sad atmosphere, filling people's hearts with a strong visual impact.

This great painting has been exhibited in more than 30 countries including the United States, Germany, France, the United Kingdom, the Netherlands, and Sweden, and it has attracted worldwide attention. After seeing this painting, Daisaku Ikeda, a Japanese writer, wrote to the painter, "The moment I watched the painting of *Nanjing Massacre*, my heart skipped a beat, and it was bleeding. It ignited my anger... We will never forget the extreme atrocities of the Japanese army... We must fight resolutely with the move that some self-righteous authorities are denying and distorting the brutal history, and their reckless act." However, the exhibition was obstructed and opposed by the Japanese right-wing forces when it was held in New York, Amsterdam and other cities, and the travelling exhibition in Japan in 1999 was cancelled due to the sensitive theme, but this did not prevent the author from keeping his original creation intention, speaking to the world and yelling for peace. May the Chinese people not forget the national crisis, and hope that all mankind will look forward to the future and defend peace.

Christian Poirot, a French oil-painting artist, also created an oil painting *Deliverance*, which is the biggest piece that he has created in more than 30 years. The artist had known little about the Nanjing Massacre before he heard of it by chance one day, and it shocked him and inspired his creativity. Then, he specifically looked up historical resources about the Nanjing Massacre, visited the memorial hall, and spent 6 months working on it. On this huge tarpaulin, Japanese invaders in yellow military uniforms were wielding their sabers mercilessly; the painful and distorted images and gushing blood of the victims were accusing the cruelty of the war; the innocent victims turned into white doves flying into the sky, symbolizing a kind of liberation and hope for peace. This painting was donated to the Memorial Hall of the Victims in Nanjing Massacre by Japanese Invaders in 2015 for exhibition. Christian Poirot hopes to let more Westerners understand the Nanjing Massacre through his oil painting, which can facilitate their comprehension of this history.

In addition, with the ever-increasing cultural exchanges and technological development, Nanjing also commemorates this history in the form of symphony concerts, poem recitations, song creation, dance creation, and drone performances. Art can serve as a means to resolve conflicts, for it can preserve history, express the artist's opinions on the historical events and convey his feelings for them. To a certain extent, art can transcend national and language boundaries, and thus it can work as an important means for peace-building. Using different art forms to express condolences for the victims of the Nanjing Massacre reflects that Nanjing residents cherish peace and have a longing for a better life.

On January 27, 2016, the UN Secretary-General Ban Ki-moon specifically stressed in his speech on the International Holocaust Remembrance Day, "By remembering the victims and honoring the courage of the survivors and those who assisted and liberated them, we annually renew our resolve to prevent such atrocities and reject the hateful mentality that allows them." This is the core value that people follow in building the memory of the Nanjing Massacre during that period. Whether they are memorial venues, academic research, or literature, film and television, painting, and various art works, they try their best to show historical facts, protect historical memory of the survivors, and enhance the authenticity of the historical memory. The Nanjing Massacre is regarded as a symbol of war atrocities, warning of inhumanity of war. That period of history should not only be remembered by the Chinese people, but also by people all over the world.

Maurice Halbwachs once said in his book *On Collective Memory* that the traumatic mark would make memory more in depth. It is often said that only by remembering the tribulation, can tragedy never repeat itself. Only by keeping the historical truth in mind, can justice be maintained. However, re-examining this special historical heritage, people gradually realized that peace-building is also a way of memory. The war itself is a traumatic memory mixed with degradation, antagonism, and agony. If memory is spread in peace discourse, it is conducive to arouse the understanding and attention of others, and then a common human memory will come into being. Nevertheless, there are urgent issues that need to be considered and resolved in the future, that is, how to transcend the historical trauma, bridge the gap and heal the wounds between nations as soon as possible, prevent hatred from lasting in future generations, and promote the realization of inter-state reconciliation and peaceful development goals.

Chapter 4
Another Choice for Peace

In 2000, when the new era started, the United Nations held the Millennium Summit. During the summit, 189 countries signed the "United Nations Millennium Declaration" and formally pledged that "We will spare no effort to free our peoples from the scourge of war, whether within or between States…" It was also this year that "Peace Studies" were officially introduced into China.

History cannot be changed and decorated at will. Justice and truth are prerequisites for reconciliation, and they also provide the seeds for peace-building. Whether this seed can eventually grow into a tree of peace depends on our choice and memory. If we choose to remember with pain and hatred, the resulting violence may destroy the hard-won peace today, and may even uproot the tree of peace and completely destroy it. If we choose the path of peace, justice and truth may gain more attention and recognition, and the tree of peace will bear fruit.

As a war-torn city Nanjing was, the humiliation and trauma brought by the war penetrated into the bones of the people, but peace and development are the themes in the new era as globalization comes, and this traumatic memory has also been endowed with more significance and mission. After years of fighting for justice and peace, Nanjing at this time, like other peace-loving cities in the world, cherishes and yearns for peace to a greater degree, and turns this longing for peace into a noble responsibility for peace-building, and spares efforts to build an "international city of peace". Meanwhile, peace studies have grown out of nothing in China, and then have taken root. Nanjing has become the center of Peace Studies in China.

Initiating Peace Studies in China

Peace Studies is a new discipline that emerged after World War II. It is an interdisciplinary academic field focusing on exploring how to achieve peace through peaceful means, with the ultimate goal of building a world with more justice and peace. In 1959, the famous scholar Johan Galtung set up the International Peace Research Institute in Oslo, Norway, and served as its director. Five years later, he launched *Journal of Peace Research*, which was the first journal on Peace Studies, marking that this discipline had its own systematic approaches. Since then, international Peace Studies has extended to countries in Europe, America, Asia and Africa, and gradually the academic sphere and discipline system of Peace Studies come into being.

Peace Studies in China originated in 2001, when the World History of the History Department of Nanjing University and the Center for Peace and Reconciliation Studies (Now known as "Centre for Trust, Peace and Social Relations") of Coventry University started formal cooperation. Nanjing and Coventry have similar traumatic memories and they, together with Dresden in Germany and Hiroshima in Japan, are known as the world's four major "martyr cities" during World War II. Coventry treats and deals with the trauma of war in the way of "reconciliation and forgiveness", and has established this Peace Studies Center at Coventry University. The two universities jointly designed a Sino-British university cooperation project for Peace Studies. Each year, 1-2 teachers from Nanjing University, funded by the British Council, are sent to Coventry University for systematic study of the main course of Peace Studies.

When Chinese scholars were introduced to Peace Studies, they immediately became interested in its unique insights into war, violence, social injustice, and gender differences. For example, when "peace" was talked about in the past, the first thought that came into people's mind would always be of no war. But according to the theories of Peace Studies, peace is not just the absence of war, but is acquired positively through eliminating hunger, violence, violation of human rights, refugee issues, global environmental pollution and other threats. It means to create a social environment where people can live a prosperous life and live in dignity, which is called positive peace. Peace Studies emphasizes the use of non-violent means to achieve the goal of conflict resolution through conflict transformation.

China is a country with a very early civilization and a long history. The Chinese history and culture include rich concepts of peace. The thought of peace has also been one of the mainstreams of traditional Chinese culture for thousands of years. After the founding of New China, many teaching practices have actually promoted peace education. And China's diplomacy has always adhered to the Five Principles of Peaceful Coexistence, as well as the current "One Belt, One Road" initiative and the great practice of building a community with a shared future for mankind, which demonstrate China's peaceful and friendly attitude. Therefore, the vigorous development of Peace Studies in China is of great significance both to China and the world. It was with this kind of thinking and responsibility that Professor Liu Cheng was determined to take the lead in promoting the peace studies in China's universities after he finished his study and returned from Coventry. As a city with its unique background of peace, Nanjing has come out from the trauma and has become the place to set sail for China's Peace Studies.

Introduction of Books on Peace Studies

In 2003, the first book on peace studies was published in China, and it was *Justice and Reconciliation: After the Violence*, written by Andrew Rigby. Then, two books were introduced, translated and published in China, *Peace by Peaceful Means: Peace and Conflict, Development and Civilization* by Johan Galtung, and the other, *Peace and Conflict Studies*, a most famous course-book, co-authored by David P. Barash and Charles P. Webel. They have opened a window for Chinese scholars to know about Peace Studies.

Nanjing University is universally recognized as the research center of Peace Studies in China. So far, it has organized and published over 30 books on Peace Studies, including *Peace Studies*, the first textbook on Peace Studies for college and university students, which was compiled according to the lecture notes of the Peace Studies course at Nanjing University, the first translation series of Peace Studies, the first set of readers on Peace Studies for primary and secondary school students, and the first research series of traditional Chinese thoughts on peace.

In 2008, the "Translation Series of Peace Studies" was published with a total of 8 books. This series of books covers a wide range of topics, including hot issues like the new paradigm of Peace Studies, globalization, environment, humankind, energy, food and health, water safety, introducing the latest international research results on Peace Studies. The next year, a set of readers on Peace Studies of "Growth in Peace" for primary and secondary school students was published. This series is composed of three volumes, including pictures and texts, which are easy to understand. Among them, the book *Love and Peace* highlights the education of love and warns young people that there is no peace without love, and they should love themselves, other people, nature and the society. The book *Cognition and Peace* enables students to recognize peace, teach them conflict resolution techniques according to the physical and mental characteristics of adolescence. *Responsibility and Peace* expands on various issues related to peace, expounds the content and methods of building peace and eliminating violence, and points out the responsibility of individuals in realizing the ideal of peace. This series was selected as one of the 100 excellent books recommended by the General Administration of Press and Publication to young people across the country in 2010.

In 2015, the bilingual *Peace-Building in a Globalized World: An Illustrated Introduction to Peace Studies*, written by Liu Cheng and Egon Spiegel, professor of University of Vechta in Germany, was published with parallel Chinese and English texts. A lot of pictures are used in the book, together with Chinese and English explanations, systematically expounding the basic concepts and cutting-edge issues of peace research and conflict resolution in the international academia. In the preface of this book, Professor Johan Galtung wrote, This extraordinary book is global peace studies! The book itself builds peace in a globalizing world, written in two major world languages, and co-authored by authors also spanning the Orient-Occident gap. The book not only has a message, but it is a message. The message is strong, with a rich combination of many ideas. And underlying it is the greatest gift of all—optimism.

In 2018, it was the 40th anniversary of the signing of the Treaty of Peace and Friendship between China and Japan. On the eve of the National Memorial Day, 5 sets of 12 books were released at Memorial Hall of the Victims in Nanjing Massacre by Japanese Invaders. These sets of books include not only historical research on the facts of the Nanjing Massacre, the latest-discovered historical archives, and the war memories from a third-party perspective, but also books that show the history of non-governmental exchanges between China and Japan. For example, *A Journey of Peace: The Oral History by the Japanese Friends*, was organized and published according to the interview of 10 Japanese guests, including Lin Boyao, Matsuoka Tamaki, and Akimoto Yoshiaki. They told about their relationship with the history of the Nanjing Massacre from different perspectives, showing the development and changes of the cause of Sino-Japanese friendship. Another unique book, *In Search of Reconciliation between China and Japan*, was co-authored by British Basil Scott and Japanese Minoru Kasai, both of whom spent their childhood in China during World War II and witnessed the bloody scene brought about by that war. The two, wounded by World War II, had special and deep feelings for China, so decades later, when they met unexpectedly in India, driven by their special love for China, the two devoted all their lives to the improvement of Sino-Japanese relations, and decided to write down this precious historical memory. Basil Scott frankly stated at the book's press conference, "Reconciliation is difficult for any person and either country, and we need to make major changes in our hearts to reconcile."

Meanwhile, researchers of China's Peace Studies are also actively conducting international exchanges. As early as 2005, the Department of World History of Nanjing University and the Center for Peace and Reconciliation of Coventry University jointly organized the first international conference on China's Peace Studies in Nanjing and more than 60 scholars attended it. Since then, Nanjing University has successively held four international peace seminars in Beijing, Xi'an, Harbin and Xiangtan in cooperation with local universities or non-governmental organizations. These conferences invited scholars of Peace Studies from China and abroad to jointly study historical and practical issues, share the latest research results, and lay a good foundation for China's Peace Studies and for academic exchanges.

Fig.4-1 Some Monographs and Translations of Peace Studies

Looking for a "Key to Sino-Japanese Reconciliation"

As a practice-oriented discipline, Peace Studies is supposed to meet the real needs of the social development. The development of Nanjing cannot avoid the historical issues involved with China and Japan, the relations of which are also one of our biggest concerns. According to John Paul Lederach, the core elements of reconciliation include peace, truth, justice, and forgiveness. Reconciliation is a process in which the above four elements are combined. Justice and forgiveness are the two basic elements of Sino-Japanese reconciliation, which is also an interactive process. Therefore, reconciliation is in fact an interdependent thought and force, and a process, which means that people creatively realize the transformation of conflicts with the joint efforts of all parties.

In order to promote peace and reconciliation between China and Japan, a peace dialogue mechanism was established in 2015. The first session of peace dialogues between Chinese and Japanese scholars was held in Beijing with the theme of the "Past, Present, and Future of Relations between China and Japan". The meeting reiterated the meaning of peace and renunciation of the war, and emphasized that the Chinese and Japanese people, like other people in the world, love peace and oppose war. The entire process of the conference was broadcast live by the media on the web, reflecting the openness of this dialogue, and laying a good foundation for the subsequent peace dialogue between the Chinese and Japanese academic circles.

At the beginning of 2017, the second peace dialogue between Chinese and Japanese scholars was held in Nanjing as scheduled with the theme of "A New Vision for Peace in East Asia". [Fig.4-2] Nearly 50 experts in Peace Studies from China and Japan opened up an in-depth discussion on the possibility of peace cooperation between the two countries. At the meeting, the "Nanjing Consensus" was jointly issued by Chinese and Japanese scholars, who expressed that it was necessary to face up to the history, remember the painful

Fig.4-2 The Second Peace Dialogue between Chinese and Japanese Scholars

lessons of the war, and make every effort to prevent the tragedy of war from recurring. It was necessary to treat each other frankly, deepen people-to-people dialogue and exchanges, and consolidate the foundation of mutual trust and friendship between the Chinese and Japanese peoples. It was necessary to look to the future, strengthen the the youth cultivation, and sow the seeds of friendship between the two nations for generations to come. It was necessary to maintain peace, foster a sense of community with a shared future for mankind, and contribute to East Asia and world peace. It was the 45th anniversary of the establishment of normal diplomatic relations between China and Japan, and the 80th anniversary of the Nanjing Massacre in 2017, when it would provide impetus for maintaining the prosperity and stability of East Asia through such a peace dialogue.

After a lapse of two years, the third peace dialogue between Chinese and Japanese scholars with the theme of "Envisioning a New Era in East Asia: The Potential for Sino-Japanese Peace Studies" was held in Osaka, Japan in 2019. Unlike previous single academic dialogues, this session had rich content, including keynote speeches, keynote reports, round table workshops, field visits, etc. Representatives of China and Japan focused on three themes, the "Japanese historical issue", "status of East Asia and the Korean peninsula issue" and "development of the discipline of Peace Studies", conducted all-round exchanges, and achieved a high degree of consensus on the future academic exchanges and peace education cooperation between China and Japan.

Starting from the first China-Japan dialogue hosted by the non-governmental organization, the second China-Japan dialogue evolved into a joint cooperation between the civil society organization and the government, and was convened by the Memorial Hall of the Victims in Nanjing Massacre by Japanese Invaders, showing China's distinctive stand to treat history, and her support for the cause of peace. The third China-Japan dialogue was jointly convened by five organizations of China and Japan, including the UNESCO Chair on Peace Studies at Nanjing University. The change from a participant to a co-organizer by the Japanese side not only reflected the Japanese scholars' recognition of the dialogue events, but also reflected the influence of Nanjing after it became one of the international cities of peace.

The fundamental improvement of Sino-Japanese relations is bound to be a long-term interactive process. According to Peace Studies, once a certain image is formed in a certain group, it often becomes a fixed existence. The enemy contains a deeply disgusting, irritating image. When we come face-to-face again, we may reject changes and information from the other side because of our previous bias, which leads us to focus more on the drivers of conflict rather than find alternative solutions. Thus, there is a long way to reconciliation.

One of the goals of peace-building is to promote mutual understanding and trust, in which civil factor and public opinion play a crucial role. The China-Japan peace dialogue between scholars of the two countries is supposed to attract more scholars, government officials, and the common people to join in, build a bridge of communication, jointly find a key to open the door of reconciliation, and to build a positive relationship for the two countries in the future.

UNESCO Chair on Peace Studies

In 2017, the "UNESCO Chair on Peace Studies" (hereinafter referred to as "the Chair on Peace Studies") successfully settled in Nanjing University, which was a milestone for the development of China's Peace Studies. Professor Liu Cheng is the Chair holder, and he is also the only Chair holder on Peace Studies in China.

One of UNESCO's goals stipulated in the UNESCO Charter is to promote international intellectual cooperation and further world peace through education, science and culture. UNESCO Chairs, formally launched in 1992, are the main means for UNESCO to promote the exchange of experience and knowledge between universities and other higher education institutions, and support capacity building. According to the resolution of the 26th General Conference of UNESCO, the UNESCO Chairs Program was UNESCO's most important activity in the field of higher education, involving all aspects of its work, such as education, human rights, cultural development, environment, basic engineering science, communications, etc. Participants of the program mainly include universities, higher education institutions, non-governmental organizations, foundations, and companies.

United Nations Educational, Scientific and Cultural Organization

UNESCO Chair on Peace Studies
Nanjing University
People's Republic of China

Fig.4-3 The Logo of the UNESCO Chair on Peace Studies

According to the latest data, UNESCO has set up more than 800 Chairs in more than 100 member states. The goal of the Chair on Peace Studies is to establish a comprehensive system integrating research, training, information exchange and document compilation of Peace Studies, strengthen the links between research, training, policy formulation and social development, and contribute to achieving the goal of "The 2030 Agenda for Sustainable Development".

The establishment of the Chair on Peace Studies indicates that peace-building in China has been recognized and affirmed by UNESCO. After having the Chair on Peace Studies, we can have closer cooperation with UNESCO in terms of resources, talents and platforms. For example, we can invite representatives of specialized agencies of the United Nations and UNESCO to participate in some activities we will organize, and use the official logos produced by UNESCO for the Chair on Peace Studies in external publicity. As a result, the influence of the peace activities by Nanjing can be better spread to the world by utilizing the Chair on Peace Studies to deepen cooperation with UN organizations at all levels.

In 2014, the first Chinese website on Peace Studies (http://unesco-peace.nju.edu.cn) was built up, and the first Chinese WeChat official account of the Chair on Peace Studies [Fig.4-4] was set up later, which was used to publish domestic and international news on Peace Studies in a timely manner, disseminate and share knowledge of peace-building and peace culture, organize Peace Studies training, and provide a good platform for cooperation and communication with international peace-loving people.

The establishment of the Chair on Peace Studies has provided new impetus for China's peace education and has been entrusted with a new mission. It targets at carrying out various forms of peace education activities, exploring peace courses covering the entire basic education, simultaneously improving individual knowledge, emotion and ability, and cultivating and popularizing peace culture. This is the only way to build peace, and Nanjing has well got it prepared.

Fig.4-4 QR Code of the WeChat Official Account of the Chair on Peace Studies

Practicing Peace Education in Nanjing

Peace education has always been the core mission of UNESCO, and it is only through education that the values of peace can be effectively transmitted. UNESCO emphasizes the role of education in the promotion of cooperation among countries to achieve world peace. In 1999, *The Declaration and Programme of Action on a Culture of Peace*, adopted by the United Nations General Assembly, stated that education is one of the key elements in building a culture of peace. Actions specific for a culture of peace include ending violence through education, dialogue and cooperation; respecting all human rights; promoting economic and environmental improvement; respecting core values such as gender rights and equality of opportunity; and respecting diversity. The culture of peace targets at ending structural violence and creating a culture of peace globally through education in values, attitudes, emotions and skills.

Peace Studies in Universities

Since 2004, Nanjing University has offered three courses on Peace Studies for undergraduates and graduates, and has begun to recruit students for master's and doctoral degrees in Peace Studies. Among them, the two courses of "Positive Peace and Conflict Transformation" and "Peace Studies: Theory and Practice", closely focusing on the culture of peace, present to students: introduction to Peace Studies, development of China's

Peace Studies, peace-building in the new era, and climate change, human rights, gender equality, structural and cultural violence, principles of negotiation, conflict transformation, etc. These courses attract more than 200 students to attend each year. So far, more than 3,000 students from different faculties have a general understanding of Peace Studies. Through these courses, many students have changed their previous views on peace and violence, have begun to pay attention to the multiple connotations of non-violence and peace, and have taken the initiative to apply the concept of peace to their study and life.

As a well-known institution of higher learning and a frontier for the promotion of Peace Studies in China, Nanjing University has invited many renowned scholars on Peace Studies in the world to Nanjing for academic exchanges in recent years, sharing the latest research results and theoretical knowledge of Peace Studies with teachers and students. Nevertheless, the promotion of Peace Studies cannot be done by one person, nor can a university. More and more colleges and universities in China have joined the "circle of friends" of Peace Studies, such as Nanjing Normal University, Nanjing Audit University, and Hunan Huaihua University. At the same time, Peace Studies in China has gradually established cooperative relations with many higher education institutions around the world.

Besides, non-governmental organizations have always been the backbone of the development of Peace Studies in China. These organizations bring together professionals and volunteers in this field to regularly organize related peace activities, promote the popularization of the peace education, as well as public participation in peace activities. With the assistance of these institutions in terms of their strong social relationship and professional knowledge, China's Peace Studies has been actively developed through international conferences, international exchanges, co-organization of summer classes, and peace activities. This is especially important in the initial establishment of Peace Studies in China, when there are a large number of international colleagues of Peace Studies and domestic peace-loving "partners" who have provided long-term help to China's Peace Studies without any consideration of remuneration. For example, The United Board for Christian Higher Education in Asia has funded China's peace-building for five consecutive years. In recent years, China has become more and more aware of the importance of Peace Studies. Some enterprises, institutions and even government agencies have begun to accept and support Peace Studies. A cooperation agreement on Peace Studies was signed between Nanjing Municipal People's Government and Nanjing University in 2019, and the university also received government funding for a joint international research center. The government's effort to promote this cause is an advantageous feature of China's Peace Studies, and it has also laid a solid foundation for its future development.

Raising the Seedlings of Peace

The UN Security Council adopted Resolution 2250 on Youth, Peace, and Security (YPS) in 2015. The landmark resolution recognized for the first time that "the important role youth can play in the prevention and resolution of conflicts and as a key aspect of the sustainability, inclusiveness and success of peace-keeping and peace-building efforts".

The youth are not just victims or perpetrators of violence, but creators of peace, and partners in dealing with extreme violence, and they must be included in future peace negotiations and peacebuilding. Peace must be achieved through the youth, in cooperation with them, and for the sake of them.

The youth represent the prospect of a nation, and basic education is an important foundation of the entire national education. Nanjing is always dedicated to incorporating peace into schools of basic education. As early as 2007, ten schools including Nanjing Langya Road Primary School, Lixue Primary School, and Primary School Affiliated to Nanjing Normal University and so on, were listed as "Nanjing Peace Education Schools", where peace-themed activities are supposed to be conducted according to the characteristics of the teenagers in a normal education manner, as well as their educational resources inside and outside the schools. In 2014, the Memorial Hall of the Victims in Nanjing Massacre by Japanese Invaders, following the experience and practices of the Polish Auschwitz Concentration Camp National Museum, the Israeli Holocaust Memorial Museum, and the Hiroshima International Peace Academy, set up a non-profit school, Nanjing International Peace School, to make use of its resources to support peace education for the primary school students.

Fig.4-5 Poster for the "International Understanding and Peace Education" of Nanjing Ninghai High School

In March 2021, the first peace education course in China, "International Understanding and Peace Education", was provided in Nanjing Ninghai High School. This was also the first experimental peace education course in a high school in China that incorporated situational experience. The course content includes an introduction to Peace Studies, diversified cultures, conflict resolution, sustainable development, etc. Senior high school students soon will grow up to be adults, and need to shoulder social responsibilities. It is conducive for them to behave in their future work and life, or to deepen their study of history when they can at this stage receive international peace education, open their international view, shape correct values and outlook on life, learn to tolerate and resolve conflicts. And almost at the same time, the course of "Growth in Peace" was also successfully offered in the junior high school of Nanjing No. 29 Middle School, which marks that peace education has officially entered the junior high school classrooms in Nanjing. This course allows students to understand the core concepts of Peace Studies through an entertaining-teaching model, to master the basic skills to resolve interpersonal conflicts, and to get improved and grow up in peace.

The immersion classroom learning brings a different experience to the intense study life of middle school students. Different from traditional classroom teaching, a lot of scenario simulations and outdoor investigations were added to this peace class, making students acclaim "history can be learned like this". For example, in the class of "Growth in Peace—Empathy", the teacher led the students out of the classroom and walked in the place where used to be "Nanking Safety Zone". The students learned and felt the touching stories of these international figures helping Chinese refugees in the background music of the song *Heal the World*. This kind of empathy is the psychological process of perceiving or imagining the emotions of others and experiencing their feelings. According to the theories of Peace Studies, empathy allows us to think from the standpoint of the other side. Without empathizing, there would be no great deeds done by those international friends. After a few classes of learning, the students responded enthusiastically. One student remarked that he had never known that peace was also a science. In order to achieve peace, people had to devote as much intelligence, energy and perseverance as they did in a war and other violence. Some students regarded "peace" as a sweet responsibility. One of them said, in fact, we had been on the road to peace, because peace was shining in everyone's thoughts, and going from violence to peace was the evolution, as well as the practice of the spiritual world. Although we were incapable to change the past, we would take things easy in the future.

In June 2022, the children of Nanjing Fengshang Kindergarten did a peace education activity. They have learned that they are a "peace seedling" from a short story called "Positive Peace". The peace seedlings will one day grow into big trees of peace, and will go on forever. The teachers of Nanjing Fengshang Kindergarten are conducting research on the peace curriculum for children, named "Cultivating Peace to Grow towards the Sun", in hopes that peace education can start from an early age, that children can learn to live and study in a positive and peaceful environment, and that parents learn to communicate with their children in a positive way. Moreover, Jiangsu Military Command No.1 Kindergarten, the Elementary School of Nanjing Jinling Huiwen School, Nanjing Foreign Language School have successively joined in the "School-Based Peace Education Program" initiated by the Chair on Peace Studies.

Peace Studies is a subject that faces the future. The future of the world belongs to children, and a peaceful world depends on today's young generation. When those young people who have received peace education work on various positions, many long-standing conflicts will be resolved, and the world will change as a result. Young people are the key force in future peace-building. Planting the seeds of understanding, respect and peace in their hearts will be the basic needs of cultivating future citizens, that is, nurturing a culture of peace and building a spirit of peace with peace education. The development of peace education in China has broad prospects.

Diversified Peace Education

Peace Education refers to transferring knowledge about peace to students, including what peace is, why peace is not achieved, and how to achieve it. In school conflict resolution is usually taught to students about the dangers of violence and conflict, to instruct students how to deal with the conflicts. However, as the social background changes, the extension of peace education is also expanding, and many different types of peace education have emerged, such as world order studies, human rights education, non-violence research, environmental protection research, violence prevention education, and many more. There are also peace courses set up by countries and regions according to their own needs, such as "anti-nuclear education" in Japan and "education for mutual understanding" in Ireland. Although the goals of peace education may be similar, due to the efforts of peace educators to deal with different forms of violence in various social contexts, peace education takes on varied forms.

Fig.4-6 Plaque of "Base School for Peace Education"

International Peace Activities

The summer school of Peace Studies is an important part of peace activities, and it is also a major feature of China's peace activities. As of 2021, Nanjing University has successively held 7 summer school programs in Peace Studies with different themes, cooperating with colleges and universities or peace research institutions to explain the theory and concept of peace to college students, to spread the peace culture. For example, the Northeast Asia Regional Peace Education Institute (NARPI) is a well-known non-governmental organization. Nanjing University and NARPI co-organized a summer school for Peace Studies in 2014, which attracted active enrollment of university scholars, school students, members of non-governmental organizations and the public from China, the United States, Japan, South Korea, Mongolia, the Philippines and other countries and regions. The summer school lasted for two weeks and was divided into two major sessions: teaching activities and field research. Through a variety of special courses on Peace Studies and localized field trips, each student learned about Peace Studies and perceived cultural diversities at the same time. It was the first time that Nanjing University had cooperated with an international non-governmental organization to hold a peace summer school program, and it also explored the way for the subsequent running of the international peace summer school. After 5 years, relying on the UNESCO Chair on Peace Studies, Nanjing University and NARPI organized the C9 Peace Studies International Summer School, the theme of which was "International Peace Education from the Perspective of a Community with a Shared Future for Mankind". The C9 Alliance is China's first top-university alliance, which has the excellent students among the universities in the country. This summer school provided more than 100 students with rich content and diverse learning experiences in the fields of conflict reconciliation, trauma treatment, anti-racism and artistic expression, and jointly discussed diversified peace issues.

In July 2017, Nanjing University and the Institute for War, Holocaust and Genocide Studies (NIOD) in Netherlands and other institutions jointly organized a summer school of "Recalling Mass Violence and the Roads to Reconciliation in Asia and Europe" for the first time. This summer school program invited more than 30 teachers and young students from well-known universities in China and abroad, and visited historical memorial venues in Nanjing, such as the Memorial Hall of the Victims in Nanjing Massacre by Japanese Invaders and Nanjing Museum of the Site of Lijixiang Comfort Stations, focused on and exchanged the experience and development of constructing the international peace memorial venues.

In March 2019, Saeki Natsuko, professor at the Faculty of International Culture of Nagoya Gakuin University, was invited by the Chair on Peace Studies to lead 11 students to Nanjing for exchanges. During the dialogue with the students of the School of History of Nanjing University, Professor Saeki said that the reason why these senior students chose Nanjing for their graduation trip was to hope that more Japanese college students would visit historical war relics and reflect on the trauma the war has brought, and cherish the hard-won peace. She also hoped that China and Japan could carry out more activities related to the youth exchanges in the future, in order to enhance mutual understanding between the youth of the two countries and promote the reconciliation between China and Japan.

In January 2020, an unprecedented COVID-19 pandemic plunged the world into extreme panic. The Institute for Advanced Studies (IAS) in Humanities and Social Sciences of Nanjing University and the Centre for Trust, Peace and Social Relations (CTPSR) of Coventry University overcame many difficulties and successfully launched a special online summer school program on Peace Studies in July. In this special 5-day summer school program, more than 30 students from various schools of Nanjing University had an online communication with teachers from Coventry University to learn the theory of peace. In 2021, led by the Chair on Peace Studies, Nanjing University and NAPRI once again jointly administered the C9 Peace Studies International Summer School. With the successful experience of the previous time, students who signed up this time became more enthusiastic, and finally a total of 61 undergraduates were selected to participate in the study. This summer school aimed to foster students' ability on how to achieve safety and equality through activities of exchanging and sharing ideas based on the themes, such as "conflict and peace framework", "restorative justice for historical harms", "community-based conflict transformation", and "the roles of the arts, education and exhibition". Such programs will continue in the city of Nanjing, encouraging more young people to learn about peace, understand peace, and join peace activities.

2021 Summer Class of Peace Studies
NJU for C9

2021年南京大学C9和平学暑期班

Topics and Schedule：

July 12: Conflict and Peace Framework
July 13: Restorative Justice for Historical Harms
July 14: Community-Based Conflict Transformation
July 15: The Roles of the Arts, Education and Exhibition

课程安排：

7月12日：冲突与和平构建
7月13日：针对历史创伤的恢复性正义
7月14日：以共同体为基础的冲突转化
7月15日：艺术、教育与展览的和平作用

Participants（Undergraduate）：

9 students from *Tsinghua University*
9 students from *Peking University*
9 students from *Xi'an Jiaotong University*
9 students from *University Of Science And Technology Of China*
9 students from *Fudan University*
8 students from *Nanjing University*
4 students from *Zhejiang University*
3 students from *Harbin Institute of Technology*
2 students from *Shanghai Jiao Tong University*

本科生学员：

清华大学9名学生
北京大学9名学生
西安交通大学9名学生
中国科学技术大学9名学生
复旦大学9名学生
南京大学8名学生
浙江大学4名学生
哈尔滨工业大学3名学生
上海交通大学2名学生

Fig.4-7 Class Schedule for the 2021 C9 Peace Studies Summer School of Nanjing University

Peace-Oriented Transformation of Memorial Venues

The Memorial Hall of the Victims in Nanjing Massacre by Japanese Invaders is the primary memorial space for the victims of the massacre, and it is also a vital place to present and shape the national memory of contemporary China. Since 2017, the memorial hall has been committed to cooperating with think tanks to improve the exhibition content, methods and language expression, to promote the inheritance of historical memory and peace-building. It used to be the place to show disasters that people dare not look at. Today it is more like a peace ark, sailing from here to the world, spreading and sowing peace in people's minds.

Peace-Oriented Exhibition

A conspicuous statue, the "Goddess of Peace" [Fig.4-8], stands on the sward of the Peace Garden in the Memorial Hall. The figure statue, 12 meters high, is made of white marble, with its main body composed of mother, baby and peace dove. The young mother embraces the happy baby and holds the peace dove spreading its wings, which means that the Chinese people condemn war, pursue peace and development, and wish for the prosperity of mankind in the future. The sculpture is 30 meters high; there

Fig.4-8 The "Goddess of Peace" Statue

are 9 (homophone of "permanent" in Chinese) steps on the front to climb up, symbolizing the beautiful wish for the world permanent peace. The peace park is based on green, symbolizing the power of life, allowing visitors to return to tranquility from the repressed memory of war. Its design and meaning also signify the shift of the memorial hall to peace.

In 2017, the Memorial Hall launched a new exhibition of historical facts—"Human Holocaust & World Memory". The new exhibition added more micro-elements and third-party historical materials to the exhibition design and layout, and attempted to stimulate more thoughts about war and individuals, rather than giving a unified historical answer. Stepping into the preface hall, you can see more than 10,000 boxes of personal files of the victims of the Nanjing Massacre displayed in the tranquility, rather than the virtual battle scenes and the rumble of cannons. This time, silence is better than sound, and the solemn and sad emotions are immediately rendered. Then stepping down and entering the exhibition hall, you can see, under the mapping of the little star lights, the stone tablet with the number of victims, and the fragments of city wall bricks with bullet holes hanging above the tablet. On both sides is a photo wall of the survivors composed of 1,213 portraits, among which more than 1,000 black-and-white photos of the survivors who have passed away are arranged symmetrically; corresponding to them, dozens of color photos of the survivors who are still alive hang on the back wall. When a survivor passes away, the light box of his or her photo will go out.

Fig.4-9 Preface Hall of the History of the Nanjing Massacre

What's the Difference between the Peace Museum and the War Museum?

In the war museum there is only a description of the history of war, and even praise for war and violence; while in the peace museum the aim focuses on peace education, exposes the cruel truth of war, shows people's active actions in loving and protecting peace, and encourages people to be positive participants in peace-building activities. Among them, the anti-war museums, resistance museums, and peace art museums can all be called "peace museums". In addition, the specific themes or issues that the peace museum focuses on are not limited to the war, and can include other forms of violence, crime, conflict, discrimination, poverty, isolation, terrorism, environmental destruction, etc., as well as solutions to these issues and conflicts. At present, there are more than 100 peace museums in the world, such as the Herbert Art Gallery & Museum in the UK, the Pearl Harbor and the USS Arizona Memorial in the US. They emphasize that peace are easy to capture people's imagination, inspire empathy, and serve as "memorials without walls", thereby allowing the culture of peace to transcend memorial walls and create change.

A more humane display of historical materials was made in the new exhibition, and at the same time the diversity of historical materials was enhanced. For example, the glass wall around the mass graves, the original site of the massacre, was heightened and made opaque to prevent children from looking directly at the horrible remains of the victims. At the same time, multimedia techniques were fully utilized in arranging and designing the historical materials for the exhibition, such as figures to show the comparison of the national and military strengths between

Fig.4-10 Exhibition Hall of Third-Party Witnesses and Testimony

China and Japan before the war, the interactive testimony of the survivor Xia Shuqin, the films on the atrocities of the Japanese army taken by the American pastor John Magee, and the office scene of the German businessman John Rabe. Through these immersive interactive methods, visitors could perceive that period of history, and ease their fear and depression that the bloody war might bring to them. A special area for "Third-Party Witness and Testimony" was set up in the new exhibition [Fig.4-10], and the news reports, documents, photos, diaries, letters, etc., of foreign journalists remaining in Nanjing that year were displayed, restoring that period of history from the perspective of the third party.

After seeing the entire exhibition, "history", "don't forget" and "peace" are the most frequent words jotted down in the guest books of the Memorial Hall. A pupil wrote down, "Don't forget the national humiliation, love peace, and if the youth is strong, the country will be strong." A visitor from the United States remarked, "It can be forgiven, but not forgotten!" Some children used pinyin to express their understanding and desire for peace instead of the Chinese characters that were beyond their literacy. There were also some people who left their improvisations in the guest books. People expressed their memory for the victims and their wish for peace in the simplest way.

Meanwhile, the Memorial Hall constantly exploring new ways to shows the historical memory. On December 14, 2017, the first "Nanjing International Poster Biennial for Peace" [Fig.4-11] officially opened to the public, which was another new form of exhibition in the Memorial Hall. In the provisional exhibition hall of the Memorial Hall, there were more than 200 peace-themed poster works centered on the two keywords of "unforgettable" and "future". This exhibition intended to awaken historical memory using visual works that crossed the boundaries between countries, nations, languages and cultures. These artworks were solicited from nearly 30 countries and regions, including China, the United States, Germany, France, Russia, and Poland. The artists used their posters to express human understanding and consensus on peace.

This event for public welfare still continued in 2021, with the theme of "a human community with a shared future". Community includes the multiple relationships between man, things, and nature. Peace is one of the most important means of connecting all things in the world. More than 7,000 poster works were collected from designers, artists, professional teachers and students from China and foreign countries. These works, integrating symbols, culture and images, express a common vision of peace and convey it among people.

Fig.4-11 The First "Nanjing International Poster Biennial for Peace"

In order to enhance the international dissemination of the massacre facts, the Memorial Hall went abroad for the first time in 2016, to Caen, France to hold the exhibition of "Witness to 1937 Nanjing Massacre". The exhibition was based on the first-hand historical materials, such as images, photos, diaries and letters left by Westerners like Rabe, Magee, Wilson, Vautrin, Sindberg and others, who stayed in Nanjing to rescue refugees, to tell the history of the Nanjing Massacre from the perspective of a third party. The reason for choosing Caen was that this city was once the main battlefield of the Battle of Normandy and also suffered the trauma of World War II. Although the two cities are tens of thousands of miles apart, the similar memories of war are empathetic, and they share a common desire for peace. After the exhibition, the Memorial Hall and Caen Peace Memorial Museum reached further cooperation in holding exhibitions, talent cultivation, and cultural exchanges. The Memorial Hall also held exhibitions in more than 30 cities around the world, including San Francisco, Nagoya, Florence, and Moscow. At the same time, it has organized many bilingual exhibitions in both Chinese and English to promote international exchange and cooperation and build a common human memory.

Being a Seed of Peace

"Being a seed of peace and bringing peace to the world" has been the most frequent words in the volunteer activities of the Memorial Hall in recent years. In 1939, the Japanese anti-war activist Jyotaro Yamaguchi brought back to Japan some orychophragmus violaceus that were growing under Purple Mountain, named them "Zijincao" (purple flowers), and he became the first messenger to sprinkle the seeds of peace between China and Japan to the world. For decades after the war, Jyotaro Yamaguchi and his family devoted themselves to planting this flower universally, preaching peace, and donating the seeds of purple flowers to schools, parks, and communities all over Japan for free, finally making this little purple flower bloom all over the Japanese archipelago.

Although the purple flower is a small plain flower, the spirit it contains is of much nobility. Today, "purple flower" has become a symbol of Sino-Japanese friendship. In April 2009, a bronze statue of the "Purple Flower Girl", donated by a Japanese friend and created by the famous Chinese sculptor Wu Xianlin, was settled in the Peace Park of the Memorial Hall. The statue of an 8-year-old Nanjing girl, 1.17 meters high, stands on a rock surrounded by purple flowers, looks at the war-torn world with her eyes wide open. The advocate, Mr. Yutaka Yamaguchi, said that his father, before his death in 1966, left his last word for him to continue the cause of spreading purple flower to promote peace. He has been doing this work for a great number of years.

Inspired by the story of purple flowers, Yakusoku, a Japanese peace activist, not only adapted it into the chorus suite *The Story of Purple Flowers*, but organized a chorus and named it the Purple Flower Chorus, which attracted more than 1,000 peace-loving people to participate. The chorus gives performances many a time in Tokyo, Kyoto and other cities in Japan. In 2001, the Purple Flower Chorus came to Nanjing for its debut performance there. So far, it has given more than 1,000 performances in Beijing, Shanghai, Harbin, Taizhou, Taipei and other cities in China. Since 2014, the Purple Flower Chorus has sent its members to Nanjing to participate in the National Memorial Ceremony every

Fig.4-12 Purple Flower, a Symbol of Peace

year. Yakusoku said, "History cannot be forgotten. We sing of purple flowers to let more people remember the history, understand the history in the right way, and express their wishes for peace at the same time." Chen Zhengrong, a Nanjing writer, said he has been tracking the story of purple flowers for more than 20 years, and has traveled to Japan many times to interview the descendants of Jyotaro Yamaguchi and the members of the Purple Flower Chorus. This story was then written into a novel of *Purple Flowers* and a long documentary literature of *The Purple Flowers under Purple Mountain*.

At the same time, the Memorial Hall created a series of activities with the purple flower as a peace symbol, like publishing the "purple flower" series of books, setting up Purple Flower Volunteer Service Team, running Purple Flower International Peace School, giving Purple Flower Peace Lectures, developing "Purple Flower" series of creative cultural products, awarding the Purple Flower International Peace Medal to the international friends who rescued people during the Nanjing Massacre.

The Purple Flower Volunteer Service Team was set up in 1994. At present, there are more than 20,000 registered volunteers and the accumulated service time exceeds one million hours. Every volunteer, like a "gardener of purple flowers", is sowing seeds of peace. Among these volunteers, there are some survivors and the descendants of the victims of the Nanjing Massacre, college students who utilize their spare time to participate in the activities, and foreigners from the United States, France, South Korea, and Japan. It is the same peace belief that brings them together. In the Memorial Hall, volunteers serve visitors from all over the world, and play a role in historiography, interpretation, caring for the survivors, theatrical performances, and promotion work; outside the memorial hall, they walk into communities and schools, nursing homes, etc., convey the voice of peace and pray for peace through public welfare activities. "A spark of light can turn into a torch, which lights the path where great love moves forward." Volunteers of Purple Flower Volunteer Service Team convey the voice of peace through their practical actions, calling on more people to join the cause of maintaining peace.

In order to popularize historical knowledge to the public, Nanjing Purple Flower International Peace School was set up by the Memorial Hall in 2017. This nonprofit school, recruiting students from all over the world, holds lectures by experts, invites survivors to give testimony on the spot, sets up special training camps and research study classes, etc., to help students deeply understand and think about that period of history. Every year, the Peace School would hold tens of teaching programs, attracting young people of different countries to participate in the study. On this basis, the Memorial Hall also organized the Purple Flower Peace Lectures, and specially invited experts and scholars in China on the Nanjing Massacre history to give lectures. Citizens could sign up online and then listen to them on the spot for free.

Assisted with the image and language of the purple flowers, people will come to visit the Memorial Hall, put on a purple flower badge, and take home a purple flower bookmark... In this simple way, more people are attracted to join the action of "Remembering History and Cherishing Peace". Let this flower of peace be integrated into one's daily life and let peace take root in their heart. The Memorial Hall is a concentrated demonstration of national will and national memory. As a "field of memory" in the history of the Nanjing Massacre, the Memorial Hall is a vital site for people to get access to that period of history. Its transformation to peace also reflects the shift of people's understanding and memory of that period of history: it is gradually evolving from the demonstration of macro-historical facts to the attention to individual fate; from the exploration of historical truths to deepening the discussion of peace-building; from the memory of war in Chinese history to the concern for a community with a shared future for mankind. This is like the last words of the late Nanjing Massacre survivor Li Xiuying left, "Remember that period of history, rather than hatred". The whole world should understand and keep in mind the truth of that period of history, but peace-building is the best memorial way.

Chapter 5

Continuing Peace-Building in the Future

China has been a peace-loving country since ancient times. More than 2,000 years ago, the view of "harmony makes everything" was put forward by the Chinese. Rich connotations of peace are reflected from views either in "harmony is precious" and "harmony with difference" advocated by Confucianism, or "not showing power to the world with military force" advocated by Taoism, or "universal love" and "defensive war" emphasized by Mohism. The idea of peace has long been deeply rooted in Chinese culture and has become an important spiritual element in shaping the peace character of the Chinese nation. Although the war left Nanjing with indelible traumatic memories, it also brought the city closer to peace. Through the unremitting efforts of all walks of life, the elements of urban peace have been excavated from the profound history, and peace has become the inherent temperament and unremitting pursuit of Nanjing.

Official Recognition that citizens of the following have self-defined their community as an International City of Peace:

Nanjing, China

A City of Peace, as officially defined by International Cities of Peace, is a community that endeavors toward progress against violence and in fostering a culture of peace.

As a guideline, United Nations Resolution A/RES/52/13 defines a Culture of Peace as a set of values, attitudes, modes of behavior and ways of life that reject violence and prevent conflicts by tackling their root causes to solve problems through dialogue and negotiation among individuals, groups, and nations.

- Foster a culture of peace through education
- Promote sustainable economic and social development
- Promote respect for all human rights
- Ensure equality between women and men
- Foster democratic participation
- Advance understanding, tolerance and solidarity
- Support participatory communication and the free flow of information and knowledge
- Promote international peace and security

Member of Advisory Council and main contact for the Initiative:

Mr. Liu Cheng
Zhang Jianjun

Executive Director   **Date:** Sept. 7, 2017

Fig.5-1 Certificate of International City of Peace

On September 4, 2017, Nanjing was accepted as the 169th international city of peace by International Cities of Peace, and it became the first city of this kind in China. [Fig.5-1] After it has become an international city of peace, Nanjing will enable the world to learn more about the long tradition of the Chinese nation's love and pursuit of peace, as well as China's efforts in peace-building. We take in the power of peace from history, narrate history in a tone of peace, and spread it in a manner of peace, so that more people will remember this painful history. This is the reason why Nanjing choose to build peace.

International Cities of Peace

International Cities of Peace is a non-profit association mainly responsible for the recognition and selection of international city of peace, and it is also the only one officially recognized by the United Nations. As of August 2022, there are over 300 international cities of peace in the world, mainly in South America, North America, Southeast Asia, Africa and Europe. Many famous cities in the world, such as Coventry in the UK, Philadelphia in the United States, The Hague in the Netherlands, Berlin in Germany and Dubai in the UAE were all granted the membership of International Cities of Peace. Inspired by Nanjing, Weifang (Shandong) and Zhijiang (Hunan) were also successively granted the membership by International Cities of Peace in 2021.

A Peace-Loving Nation

The Chinese nation loves peace and has a long history of peace culture. "Though it is powerful, a warlike country will perish" has been China's motto since ancient times. There are many ideas of peace contained in Confucianism, Taoism and Buddhism. Confucianism advocates the idea of "benevolence". "Benevolence" equals love. Starting from "benevolence", from "loving family members" to "loving more people", from "loving more people" to "loving human beings", so that mutual understanding, respect, tolerance and friendship between people are achieved. Taoism emphasizes "harmony". The *Tao Te Ching* says: "Man follows the laws of earth; earth follows the laws of heaven; heaven follows the laws of Tao; Tao follows the laws of its intrinsic nature." Lao Tzu's emphasis on "governance by inaction" is essentially against war, because war is a destruction of natural and social order, and people should be "willed to eat, dress beautifully, live in peace, and enjoy their customs…" Buddhism has always been compassionate, sympathetic to all living beings, opposed to violence and social unrest, advocates the spirit of tolerance, humility, understanding, and peace, and pursues friendship between people, friendship between nations, and reciprocity between countries, so that world peace is achieved.

Over thousands of years, China has followed a peaceful and stable development policy. General Secretary Xi Jinping said at the symposium commemorating the 75th anniversary of the victory of the Chinese People's War of Resistance against Japanese Aggression and the World Anti-Fascist War, "After modern times, the Chinese people were invaded, humiliated, and plundered by foreign powers for more than a hundred years, from which what the Chinese people have learned not the gangster logic, but the determination to maintain peace." "The past will not be forgotten, but a guide to the future. We commemorate the victory of the Chinese People's War of Resistance against Japanese Aggression and the World Anti-Fascist War, condemn the brutality of the aggressors, and emphasize bearing in mind the historical experience and lessons. It is not to perpetuate hatred, but to arouse kind-hearted people's yearning and perseverance for peace. It is to take history as a mirror and face the future, cherish and maintain peace together, and let the people of China and Japan continue to be friendly from generation to generation, and people from all over the world enjoy peace and tranquility forever."

History has proved that peace-loving countries can finally achieve peace. In comparison with other ancient civilizations, Chinese civilization has been able to survive to this day because we believe that peace is more powerful than brutal violent conquest. Not long after the founding of New China, the Chinese government put forward the Five Principles of Peaceful Coexistence. As the largest developing country, China adheres to the neighboring foreign policy that emphasizes good neighborliness and partnership with neighbors, constantly consolidates friendly cooperative relations with them, and builds a community based on mutual benefit and interests. China actively conducts multilateral diplomacy and international cooperation. It has participated in almost all important international organizations and played an important role in multilateral international mechanisms, such as arms control, trade and investment, public health, global education, and counter-terrorism. In recent years, General Secretary Xi Jinping proposed "building a community with a shared future for mankind", jointly building the "Belt and Road", strengthening dialogue among civilizations, and advocating the Silk Road spirit of "peaceful cooperation, openness and inclusiveness, mutual learning, mutual benefit and win-win results". It reflects the wisdom of the Chinese nation in the long-term exchanges of civilizations, and points out the direction for promoting the progress of human civilization and the peaceful development of the world.

Fig.5-2 Nanjing Today

Nanjing has always been an important place for multicultural exchanges and it has a very rich cultural heritage. More than 1800 years ago Buddhism was introduced to Nanjing; the site of the Grand Baoen Temple is the oldest and best-preserved Buddhist temple in the history of China. The ancient Jiming Temple, a royal temple built in the Western Jin Dynasty, attracts endless stream of pilgrims throughout the year, and it has long since been known as the "first temple in the Southern Dynasties". The traditional Buddhist thought carries on the Chinese culture of peace, and Buddhism achieves harmony in interpersonal relationships through the purification of individual minds and the living environment of the community. More than 400 years ago, Catholicism was also introduced to this city, and now Nanjing is the world's largest base to print Bible. Christianity also reflects peace. In the New Testament, Jesus preached "to love your enemies", because if you can't let go of your hatred in your heart and retaliate against your enemy, it will hurt you more than it hurts others.

Nanjing used to be the source and anchorage of Zheng He's voyages to the West, as well as a node city on China's Maritime Silk Road. More than 600 years ago, the navigator Zheng He set off from Nanjing for seven ocean voyages. Wherever his fleet of ships arrived, he mediated contradictions and quelled conflicts; at the same time, he exchanged special products with the countries he went to, boosted trade, and deepened friendship, leaving behind the good impression of China's friendly communication with the people of other countries along the way. Mr. Sun Yat-sen, a famous historical figure in Nanjing, took the freedom of the masses as his mission all his life. The Chinese characters "bo ai" written by him were engraved upright in the center of the stone archway of his mausoleum. Sun Yat-sen's "fraternity" primarily meant loving the Chinese nation and the Chinese compatriots. It was also his lifelong political goal to promote love, development, and progress for all people around the world, and it reflects Nanjing's spirit of peace.

Nanjing, capital of Jiangsu Province, is vibrant and open, making it a central city of contemporary China. As an important central city in eastern China, as well as a mega-city in the Yangtze River Delta, with a permanent population of nearly 9.5 million, of which teenagers account for about 20%. In 2021, there are around 900,000 university students in Nanjing, so it is also known as a veritable "City of Youth" and "Vital City" for its leading place of higher education resources in the country. The youth represent the future of a nation, and they are the core competitive power of a city. The young people, vigorous and positive, are undoubtedly the main force in spreading a culture of peace and building peace. Moreover, Nanjing, with its unique historical and cultural facilities, such as the Ming City Wall, Confucius Temple, Qinhuai River Scenic Belt, Laomendong, Yihe Road, Nanjing Six Dynasties Museum, Chaotian Palace, and Jiangnan Shipbuilding Museum, has been continuously enriching and expanding its cultural resources of peace.

Nanjing has aspired to be an international city of peace and has gained inexhaustible power from its rich historical heritage. It hopes to become a city oriented toward positive peace and inherit this "Chinese spirit".

Actions beyond Words

Establishment of National Memorial Day

December 13 is a day that is fixed in the mind of the Chinese people, because the city of Nanjing was occupied by the Japanese army that day in 1937 and the people there began to suffer the tribulation. In order to commemorate all the victims who were killed by the Japanese invaders during the Japanese War of Aggression against China, December 13 has been established as the National Memorial Day for the Nanjing Massacre Victims since 2014, and a national memorial event has been held in the name of the country.

This day, all entertainment activities in China come to a halt, and all web pages become black and white. At 10 o'clock in the morning, the air raid warning used for wartime sounds again throughout Nanjing. Cars stop and sound their horns, and pedestrians stand still in silence, as if time had frozen. At the same time, the honor guards solemnly present 8 wreaths on the memorial service altar in the melody of the *National Memorial Service Music* played by the military band at the memorial ceremony held in Nanjing, to express the mourning of the whole nation to the victims in the massacre and to pay tribute to the revolutionary martyrs and national heroes who gave their lives for the victory of the Chinese People's

War of Resistance against Japanese Aggression. [Fig.5-3] After the ceremony, the youth representatives of Nanjing read the "Declaration of Peace" and then rang the "Peace Bell". With three deep bells, thousands of peace doves representing the lives of the victims spread their wings into the blue sky.

At the National Memorial Ceremony in 2017, 80 youth representatives from Nanjing read the "Declaration of Peace", which contains over 200 characters. It was written by Feng Yitong, referring to the rhyme style of the Chinese classic *The Book of Songs*, the style of which features in every sentence including four characters, and reads catchy. It enhances and puts in the feelings for Nanjing, for the tragic history and the wish for peace. In the declaration, it reads, "When the great principle is prevailing, all under heaven will be equal; when the great kindness is shown to all, the harmony will make an auspicious world", signifying that staying away from war and cherishing life, only peace can bring harmony and happiness.

Fig.5-3 National Memorial Ceremony for the Victims of the Nanjing Massacre

Formally holding memorial commemorations and service in the name of the country, on the one hand, is to respect the deceased and feel awe at life; on the other hand, it also contributes to the identification of national feelings and that of collective memory. The discourse power of the national memorial service will be conducive to keep this historical memory in an awakening state for a long time, and at the same time will counterattack those who vainly deny and distort that period of history in the world, demonstrating China's firm stand in safeguarding the historical truth. The Massacre Memorial Day was established to demonstrate to the world the Chinese nation's attitude towards human rights and civilization, and the Chinese people's wish and responsibility to maintain peace together with the people of the world. The national commemorations and memorial service also warn people of the whole country not to forget the lives lost in the wars, not to forget the precious peace, not to forget the catastrophe the country suffered, and make the country strong!

Nanjing citizens have also spontaneously organized and participated in various activities to commemorate the victims of the compatriots, such as going to the memorial places for silently mourning, bowing, offering flowers, and paying a visit. On the National Memorial Day, every elementary, middle school and university in Nanjing will spontaneously mourn the victims and pray for world peace in forms of having "candlelight memorial service", reciting poems, making paper cranes, holding theme class meetings, and seeing historical documentary films. All parts of the country and the world have also joined the memorial activities in their own way. On December 13, 2020, due to the impact of the COVID-19 globally spread, many international friends failed to come to the ceremony on the spot, but through the special method of online videos, they cherished the memory of the victims in Nanjing Massacre on the National Memorial Day and prayed for peace together.

Many countries in the world have set up memorial days and memorial halls for victims in the massacres to pay tribute to those innocent civilians who were killed in the war and warn the world of the harms of war. Examples are the United Nations' International Holocaust Remembrance Day, the Day of Liberation of Auschwitz in Poland and the Holocaust Remembrance Day in Germany on the same day of January 27, and the Victory Day in the Great Patriotic War of Russia on May 9, Yom Hashoah (the Holocaust Remembrance Day) in Israel on the 27th day of Nisan, the National Pearl Harbor Remembrance Day in the United States on December 7, etc. The victims deserve to be remembered, and violence and war to be cast aside. As a large developing country, China has the responsibility to promote this memory from the national memory to the world memory, calling on the people of the world to learn from history and create the future together.

United Nations' International Holocaust Remembrance Day

In 2005, the 60th United Nations General Assembly passed Resolution 60/7, designating January 27 as the annual International Holocaust Remembrance Day to commemorate the 6 million Jewish Holocaust victims and millions of other victims by the Nazi regime. The day is to remind people not to forget that cruel history and to fight against the atrocities that led to that kind of disaster. At the same time, the United Nations also urges each member country to develop educational programs to prevent the human disaster of genocide from reoccurrence.

Aiding Africans Fight against the Epidemic

In the spring of 2020, Nanjing, just overcoming the crisis of the COVID-19 epidemic, is also paying close attention to the anti-epidemic situation in other international cities of peace in the world. On March 17, the UNESCO Chair on Peace Studies at Nanjing University (hereinafter referred to as "the Chair") sent a letter to Fred Ament, president of the International Cities of Peace. On March 22, the leaders of 13 cities of peace in Africa sent letters for help to the Chair through Mr. Ament. The city of Wamba, Nigeria, bluntly stated in the letter, "There have already been 8 suspected cases of COVID-19 in Nigeria. According to the current situation, if preventive measures are not taken, the number of cases may increase. This virus is separating husband and wife, family, and friends in our country, as well as affecting our education system. We need medical and material aid to maintain the safety of our community." Masal Chawe Education Center in Masal City, Kenya replied: "There are 258 children in the education center. 81 of them were homeless because of the sudden outbreak of the epidemic, and there is a lack of basic relief supplies here. It is difficult to ensure that these children are protected from the virus." A letter from the Monga City, Congo (DRC) wrote, "When the Ebola virus is still invading our country, people are still panicking. In Monga at the moment, our hospital does not have equipment to detect whether people have the COVID-19. We urgently need medical training, medical awareness, protective equipment…"

Behind each letter for aid was the anxiety about the epidemic and longing for living. After receiving these letters for help, the Chair immediately carried out rescue plans. The Chair sought available ways to assist Africa from relevant non-profit organizations. In the name of the "friends of the Chair on Peace Studies", a fundraising activity to aid Africans was launched. After receiving aid funds and anti-epidemic materials, such as hand sanitizer, soap, buckets, and clinical thermometers, the leaders of the local cities of peace in Africa distributed them to the residents as soon as possible. During the epidemic, an ordinary bucket could be used to build a hand-washing spot to ensure that the adults and children nearby could get clean water. At the same time, the Chair also shared the translated version of "The Coronavirus Prevention Handbook" (English, French, German versions) through the platform of the International Cities of Peace to all cities of peace in Africa and other countries, allowing them to refer to China's anti-epidemic experience to understand the epidemic and establish a sense of protection.

In this program, a total of 33 cities of peace in Africa received assistance. Mr. Fred Arment, president of International Cities of Peace, specially made a video to express his gratitude to the people of Nanjing for their assistance to Africa. After that, the Chair also cooperated with international friends to provide material assistance to the two tribes in the Amazon rainforest. The anti-epidemic activity initiated by the Chair was praised by the UNESCO headquarters and reported by many domestic and foreign news media, which has won Nanjing a good international reputation.

Fig.5-4 Poster of Nanjing's Aiding Africans Fight against the Epidemic (2020)

Joining the UNESCO Creative Cities Network as "City of Literature"

In October 2019, Nanjing was designated as a member City of Literature of UNESCO Creative Cities Network, and it also became the first city in China to receive this title. Nanjing is known as the "Cultural Hub under Heaven", where the classics handed down from generation to generation, such as *A Dream of Red Mansions*, *Yongle Canon*, *Unofficial History of the Scholars*, etc. Since modern times began, famous literary talents and masterpieces have emerged endlessly here. Familiar literary masters, such as Lu Xun, Ba Jin, Zhu Ziqing, Yu Pingbo, Zhang Henshui, and Zhang Ailing all had a special relationship with Nanjing. *The Good Earth*, the Nobel Prize award-winning work by Pearl S. Buck, was also created here. In contemporary times there are a large number of excellent writers in Nanjing. They have written unique literary works, which allow the world to know about Nanjing and China, and make diverse cultures in the world meet here with the ties of literature. Jean-Marie Gustave Le Clézio, French writer and the Nobel Prize winner, wrote in his recommendation letter for candidacy of Nanjing as a City of Literature, "Nanjing is a beautiful city… It is rich in art and history, and has a great literary heritage… and for allowing me to meet the contemporary writers who live in Nanjing and thus to discover the enthusiasm of the youth of this city for literature. During my stay in Nanjing, I have participated in many literary events and activities. Nanjing is one of the most dynamic and welcoming poles of China, not only in terms of literary creation, but also in terms of translation and publication of literary works."

Literature is an important carrier for peace-building. In literature, the experience of war is often translated into words and widely spread, recording and telling human trauma and miseries. Meanwhile, they also depict and praise peace, allowing people to feel the power and beauty of peace in words. In the context of peace studies, literature is conducive to achieve reconciliation after war in some degree because it adopts a non-violent way to express the trauma. It also has the

Fig.5-5 A Sight of the Headquarters of Pioneer Bookstore

power to promote unity and inclusion, expressing the desire to build peace in a respectable form. It can also be a means of having dialogue, understanding each other, and bridging the souls of people in the world. Peace studies emphasize communication. Communication helps us see the world through diverse and inclusive lenses, giving us the opportunity to discover more of the commonalities among people that can fill the gaps, eliminate misunderstandings and disputes that can create conflict.

Nanjing has various initiatives to encourage reading, which does honor to its inhabitants and to their literature reading. Bookstores have become the exclusive cultural space in the city. Pioneer Bookstore (Librairie Avant-Garde) is one of the famous cultural brands of Nanjing. Though a private academic bookstore founded in 1996, it was selected as one of the top ten bookstores in the world by *National Geographic* in 2016. Its advertising slogan, "The soul, a stranger on the earth", taken from the poem of the Austrian poet Georg Trakl, means that the wanderer soul sets out in search of its own homeland, where it must dwell. A good bookstore is supposed to be a homestead for the reader to rest his soul, and Pioneer Bookstore is the one of this kind. This bookstore has a unique development concept and currently has over 10 branches in Nanjing. Its headquarters, located in a former underground parking lot that had been rebuilt from the air-raid shelter of Wutaishan, does not need any gorgeous decorations for its business operation, but a clean and simple atmosphere that returns to the essential concept of the book, and it provides a cultural space for this city. [Fig.5-5] In 2021, Pioneer Bookstore rebuilt a former cement factory that was built in the 1970s into ten themed stacks, transforming the production workshops that were abandoned with the times into a cultural, creative and artistic space which is placed on the prospect of the times. As a result, this old building complex is given new vitality, and at the same time, it brings vitality as well as spiritual nourishment and healing facility to the city.

Nanjing is constantly opening up new cultural spaces. For example, Jinchuang Book City, as a commercial part of the Jinchuang Digital Industrial Park, keeps a collection of 140,000 volumes. Through exhibitions, reading clubs, creative cultural markets, social activities and so on, it integrates social and cultural resources to create a "book + X" cultural concept experience space, which includes a parent-child study room, the *Reader* salon, China-Tide culture, and so on. In addition, a Peace Theater [Fig.5-6] is specially opened to host more colorful cultural and artistic activities and social interaction.

Fig.5-6 Peace Theater of Jinchuang Book City

Construction of "Ecological Nanjing"

A state of peace is inseparable from sustainable development. The United Nations' "Transforming Our World: The 2030 Agenda for Sustainable Development", put into effect on January 1, 2016, provides an updated statement on the full implementation of the "culture of peace": We are determined to foster peaceful, just and inclusive societies which are free from fear and violence. The agenda calls on all countries to take action to achieve 17 sustainable development goals in the next 15 years. These goals address the needs of people in both developed and developing countries, and involve three dimensions of sustainable development, society, economy, and environment. This includes building more peaceful and inclusive societies and achieving economic, social and technological progress in harmony with nature. This not only contains the common vision of mankind, but also points out the direction for sustainable development.

Environmental sustainable development is crucial. Since the 18th National Congress of the Communist Party of China was held in 2012, China has also pushed environmental protection to a new height. General Secretary Xi Jinping attaches great importance to the protection of the ecological environment that "we must never sacrifice the ecological environment for temporary economic development" and "clean waters and green mountains are just as valuable as gold and silver". As an international garden city, the ecological quality and livability index of Nanjing have long been at the top of the cities all over the Yangtze River Delta, and it has been selected as one of the "China's Most Happy Cities" and "Top 10 Most Livable Cities". In 2020, it was awarded the title of "National Garden City" again. Nanjing has become a firm practitioner of environmental protection by "integrating history into nature", promoting urban scientific, green and low-carbon development.

In recent years, Nanjing has combined urban natural resources and human resources to create an urban landscape of mountains, water, city, and forest. The urban green coverage rate and forest coverage rate have reached 44.8% and 29.9% respectively. Throughout the year, you can always find green scenery in this city. During holidays, it has become a leisure habit of many Nanjing inhabitants to go to scenic spots, university campuses or parks to appreciate flowers and greenery, or take family and children to relax on the lawn. Even on both sides of the road in Nanjing, there are carefully planted colorful and layered green belts, allowing the citizens have a view of dense greenery.

Targeting at "ecological Nanjing", Nanjing has created possible scenarios and carried out the plans to rebuild dilapidated houses and shantytowns as well as the old communities, which organically reconstructs the city; to rebuild and protect historical areas, such as Yihe Road, Laomendong, Xiaoxihu, Pingshi Street, etc.; to create urban characteristic spaces along the Yangtze River, along the city wall, along the Qinhuai River, and along the historic streets; at the same time, to accelerate industrial transformation and upgrading, reduce urban pollution, and protect biodiversity. Just as General Secretary Xi Jinping said, "Let the city blend into nature, let the residents see the mountains, see the water, and remember nostalgic memories", Nanjing is working towards this goal step by step.

Fig.5-7 Green Nanjing—Nanjing Drum Tower Square

Nanjing Peace Park

Peace Park [Fig.5-8] is a representative street park in Nanjing. It is close to the Nanjing Municipal People's Government, and is only 100 meters away from the Jiming Temple Scenic Spot. It is an ideal place for residents to relax and do exercise. Although it is "Nanjing's smallest park", it is like "a sparrow, complete with five internal organs". In the park, iconic landscapes, such as the Lishi Bell Tower and Panchi, which were built in the Republic of China, are well preserved, and there are pavilions, rockeries, and flower pots for citizens to enjoy. The park also integrates the elements of peace with the Peace Statue of a maiden with a white dove, and the peace-dove decorations in the park. In 2011, more than 300 trees were removed from here due to the construction of subway line. However, with the completion of the subway line, the Nanjing Municipal People's Government decided to restore the "greening" of the park on the agenda. The green park, once lush and fragrant with birds and flowers, has not only fully restored, but also added many new species, with the old ones that have grown for decades retained, including walnut tree, metasequoia, juniper, cedar and other large tree. The connection between urban development and peace-building will be strengthened by getting close to nature, enjoying the park, and savoring peace.

Fig.5-8 Nanjing Peace Park

Collected Wisdom for Peace

In 2020, the event of the 2020 International Day of Peace was held in Nanjing. During the event, UNESCO and Nanjing signed a memorandum of cooperation and promised to hold the International Peace Forum in Nanjing for three consecutive years starting from 2020, which will become an important and normalized dialogue platform to promote knowledge and cultural exchanges, and contribute to the sharing of diverse wisdom in coping with global challenges and pushing forward sustainable peace-building.

Before hosting this peace forum, Nanjing specially sent representatives to inspect peace forums of the forerunners in the cities of other countries, for example, the Paris Peace Forum and Coventry's RISING Global Peace Forum. Among them, the Paris Peace Forum, beginning in 2018, was originally initiated by French President Macron to commemorate the centennial of the armistice of World War I, with its theme focusing on global hot issues, and involving global governance, biodiversity, inclusive economy, new technology and many other fields. The forum, held once a year, brings together governmental heads from many countries, as well as outstanding representatives in various fields such as business and academia, and is committed to providing creative solutions for the current multiple crises and challenges that the international community is facing through conflict resolution. At present, it has greater influence on a global scale. In 2020, General Secretary Xi Jinping delivered a video speech at the 3rd Paris Peace Forum, calling on all countries to unite and cooperate to fight the epidemic, adhere to green development and promote economic recovery, and safeguard world fairness, justice, peace and security. The Coventry's RISING Global Peace Forum, relying on the city's membership of the International Cities of Peace, makes full use of the Centre for Trust, Peace and Social Relations at Coventry University, Coventry City Council and Coventry Cathedral, the tripartite partnership of which combines important speeches, seminars and workshops given by high-level speakers, sets themes around the peace issues the world is currently facing and conducts dialogues on peace every year.

After fully taking in the experience of many other cities, the "Youth and Peace" dialogue, as a prelude to the activities for the 2020 International Day of Peace, was successfully held on September 21 in Nanjing. The dialogue invited representatives of UNESCO, experts and scholars as mentors to have dialogues with youth representatives from different fields from China and foreign countries on the topics like "women and children", "poverty elimination", "youth responsibility", "rural education", and "intangible heritage protection", and exchanged practical experiences. On the spot, an online relay of "Peace Book" through network was initiated from Nanjing to the world to encourage more people to truly participate in it, and to invite people from different countries and regions to give their voices to peace together through painting, music, photography, text, etc. After the dialogue, the participants shared an art performance on peace including music, poetry and dance. Young people from all over the world sang songs, recited poems, performed dance, and paid tribute in an artistic way. It was a warm-up activity for the follow-up International Peace Forum.

Fig.5-9 Logo of the First Nanjing Peace Forum

On October 24, 2020, the 75th "United Nations Day", the first Nanjing Peace Forum opened. This forum, adhering to the concept of building a community with a shared future for mankind, with the theme of "Building a Comprehensive, Diversified and Lasting Vision of Peace", brought together representatives from international organizations, experts and scholars in various fields, and representatives of young peace activists from various countries, through a combination of online and offline methods, to discuss the key factors of building perpetual peace, exchanges and mutual learning between cultures, harmonious coexistence of man and nature, and to provide suggestions for global peace-building. The layout of the venue incorporated the characteristic elements of Nanjing, such as Ming City Wall, Chinese paper folding, and "peace forest" composed of fresh green plants, and the conference preparations are impressive, using green stuff and fully highlighting Chinese characteristics. Nanjing was the main venue for this first forum, and branch venues were set up in five cities: Paris (France), Almaty (Kazakhstan), Baghdad (Iraq), Bamako (Mali), and Brasilia (Brazil), to show the world the image of Nanjing as an international city of peace and spread China's concept of peace development.

Ms. Marielza Oliveira, the representative of UNESCO to the five East Asian countries, said at the opening ceremony, "Just like the two sides of the same coin, on the one hand, the world is constantly being destroyed, and on the other hand, diplomatic relations are unceasingly developing. Nanjing underwent war fires. Negotiations led to the establishment of UNESCO. Our ultimate mission is to build peace for mankind and prevent such tragedies from happening again in any country and region in the world." This kind of peace is not just peace between nations, but peace between generations, between ethnic groups, between social classes, and economic groups, and it is the peace in all senses.

Finally, the opening ceremony started the Nanjing Peace Forum in the form of "sowing the seeds of peace", which means "let the seeds of peace take root in the hearts of the people of the world, and let the planet where we live together grow a forest of peace".

Youth play a key role in maintaining world peace and promoting reconciliation. They are the initiators of advocating peace, the creators of solutions, and the practitioners of changing the world. For this activity, we invited a group of young "buddies", who care about the world, and they are full of social responsibility, and have the ability to empathize, to share the ideas and results of peace-building and solutions. There are some who are committed to the development of fair education, and have set up a fund to care for rural children left behind; they promote women's independence and gender equality, encourage rural women to participate in community governance and construction, or provide career counseling to women in the workplace and develop their leadership. There are also efforts to eradicate poverty and connect endangered skills in remote and poor areas with the consumer market, which not only provides work opportunities for craftsmen, but also promotes traditional Chinese handicraft culture throughout the world. There was a graduate student in China from Pakistan. He took the opportunity to study in Nanjing with the help of the Chinese government scholarship,

Fig.5-10 The Manual and Badge for the First Nanjing Peace Forum

and he also used his own way to repay the society. He became the founder of FCTA (From Compassion to Action) of Nanjing Foreign Volunteer Team, which serves as a platform for young volunteers of international students to communicate. Volunteers come from different countries, with different skin colors and different languages, but they all hold the same belief, that is, to transform love into action, to contribute empathy and love to the society. The organization pays attention to rural disadvantaged children, migrant children, children of disabilities and orphans, and organizes different projects for their educational, cultural and skill development. Since its establishment in 2016, FCTA has recruited over 500 young volunteers from 60 different countries around the world, who work together to achieve the 2030 Sustainable Development Goals.

There are many such youth and groups in Nanjing. It is because of their contributions with positive energy that peace-building in Nanjing becomes possible. As we can also see, a young man with a sense of social responsibility is not only supposed to have compassion, but also to transform it into action, using his enthusiasm, kindness, and understanding of peace to make contributions to the society and the country within his capacity. Therefore, peace is not an illusory and distant dream, but a practical action!

In October 2021, the second Nanjing Peace Forum was successfully held in Nanjing. With the theme of "Harmony and Coexistence: Living in Peace with Nature", this forum brought together institutions of China and foreign countries, and youth representatives who are committed to the cause of peace-building around the world to discuss issues on international practices of peace, and actively advocate "co-existence between man and nature in peace". The opening ceremony was selected at the Nanjing Purple Mountain Music Station, which integrates the historical culture with the natural landscapes of this city. [Fig.5-11] Here, the audience enjoyed the sounds of nature, experienced the beauty of life, demonstrated the peace concept of Nanjing in the form of art, sincerely called to the world for actions and hoped to jointly protect our beautiful blue planet.

Fig.5-11 The Opening Ceremony of the Second Nanjing Peace Forum

The Nanjing Peace Forum 2021 advocates "sharing social responsibility", "sharing solutions" and "creating a sustainable future together". Experts and scholars from various fields, such as peace education, ecological protection, sustainable development, culture and art, were invited here to discuss the plan and demonstrate the significance of harmonious coexistence between man and nature. The plenary forum finally released the "Peace Consensus of Nanjing", issuing collective initiatives such as biodiversity conservation, combating inequality and discrimination, developing peace education, and jointly building a community with a shared future for mankind. At the same time, the committee of the forum put forth a proposal which was intended to be creative and problem solving, and released the solicitation of "Design for Peace" to the world, encouraging people to contribute wisdom to the cause of peace, design for peace, and work for peace. Round-table talks on the theme of "peace education" were held in the parallel forums. More than 40 representatives from education, academia, and publishing houses spoke freely at the meeting, sharing the latest research results and practical experience of peace education in China and other countries.

The successful conclusion of the forum is of great significance and it is an important node in its construction of an international city of peace. Let Nanjing become an important window for the world to perceive the peace development in China, and let it become a communication platform for global peacemakers, and an education highland for cultivating peace builders. The seeds of peace have been sown, and they are expected to grow into a forest of peace in the future by putting the concepts of peace into the minds of more people through our efforts to promote peace activities, peace education, and peace research at all levels of the society, and create more potentials for peace-building.

An Ongoing Process

Peace is not the result, but a permanent process.

In December 2016, the UN General Assembly approved a draft resolution entitled "Declaration on the Right to Peace", emphasizing that peace is an important condition for the promotion and protection of all human rights inherent to all human beings. The "Declaration on the Right to Peace" invites "solemnly all stakeholders to guide themselves in their activities by recognizing the high importance of practising tolerance, dialogue, cooperation and solidarity among all human beings, peoples and nations of the world as a means to promote peace; to that end, present generations should ensure that both they and future generations learn to live together in peace with the highest aspiration of sparing future generations the scourge of war".

The significance of peace for this city that is reborn after the war does not only lie in historical commemoration and reflection, but also in embedding the "peace gene" into its urban planning, construction, and governance by creatively using urban historical sites and public spaces to take advantage of the wide range of possibilities of peace construction where opportunities and challenges coexist.

Memorial venues, epitomizing the spirit of a city, are a vital space for the construction and inheritance of urban memories, and they are also one of the most widely used means of communication and recognition. Especially in the context of building a community with a shared future for mankind, memorial venues are supposed to serve the needs of spreading a culture of peace and creating an atmosphere of reconciliation on the basis of disseminating historical truth. Compared with the grand unitary statement of history, a narrative model that provides multiple perspectives and promotes exploratory thinking may facilitate visitors' understanding of and thinking about war and peace. For example, Yad Vashem (Israel's official memorial to the victims of the Holocaust) will play a video clip about the peaceful life of the Jewish community before the Nazis in power at the beginning of the visit, and this is in sharp contrast to the disorder and brutality caused by the advent of war, which will attract visitors' interest and develop their empathy for the victims. Another example is the Museum of Tolerance in the United States. Before entering the museum, each visitor will get a small card with a photo of a child who suffered the massacre, and "the child" will accompany the visitor all through the tour. After the visit, the card will turn into texts on the screen, telling the visitor what the child experienced that year. This interactive dialogue spanning space and time gives the visitor more subjectivity and initiative.

Peace education reflects the requirement of UNESCO to promote a culture of peace around the world, and it is also the duty of a city of peace should take. UNESCO advocates for "mainstreaming the culture of peace", and its main mission is to foster the values, attitudes and behaviors with the culture of peace, including resolving conflicts by peace, bilateral/multilateral dialogue, reaching consensus and positive non-violence, through the redesign of educational curricula. At present, a pilot program of peace education has been fully launched in Nanjing, and in the following stage, efforts will be made to improve the curriculum, compile materials for peace education, establish an evaluation system, and gradually incorporate peace education courses into the basic education curriculum system of Nanjing. Aiming at different youth groups with varied growth characteristics and combining the urban peace resources, peace education will include more topics such as social justice, environmental protection, campus violence prevention, tolerance and empathy, etc., and develop peace education courses with Chinese characteristics. Let peace studies enter classrooms, let it enter the community, carry out national citizenship education, and build peace in the minds of people.

The role of Nanjing cultural organizations, cultural facilities, and literary and artistic creation teams must be given full play of, and it is proposed to collaborate government, enterprises, schools, non-governmental organizations and religious groups in exploring the elements of peace in the city, hold peace-themed art exhibitions and recreational and sports activities, and create a good social atmosphere for the construction of an international city of peace. It is also planned to establish Nanjing International Peace Month, Nanjing International Peace Festival, and Nanjing Peace Prize, and to encourage various social resources to participate in building the city of peace in various forms. For example, the Coventry International Prize for Peace and Reconciliation was first awarded in 2000. Since then, the prize has been awarded every two years to give honors to programs, advocates, organizations or individuals who have made outstanding contributions to the promotion of peace and reconciliation or to social and environmental benefits. It is open to everyone, regardless of nationality, race or belief.

Environmental protection is also an important issue in peace-building. Nanjing has plans to create a peace-themed landscape layout. The scenarios include building a number of peace-themed parks, squares, monuments, green-plant sculptures, peace streets and other urban landscapes, protecting historical and cultural relics, planning and developing a unique cultural tourism route with the theme of peace, which will provide spatial carrier for implementing the strategy for building the city of peace and allocating peace elements. As a result, people's impression and cognition of international cities of peace will be improved. For example, the city of Coventry has combined 30 spots related to peace in the downtown area and designed a popular travel route called "Coventry Peace Trail", which starts from the ruins of the former Cathedral Church of St. Michael to Millennium Place, allowing people to experience peace along the route.

In order to encourage more people to participate in the construction of peace, it is supposed that Nanjing should rely on the platform of the International Cities of Peace to constantly expand the circle of friends of the international cities of peace, and promote the interconnection, intercommunication and mutual sharing between Nanjing and the world in the fields of science and technology, education, ecology, and innovation. At the same time, it can make full use of its unique peace culture, extracts values with universal significance from cultural products, combines academic research, paintings and calligraphy work, operas, literature, as well as traditional festivals, mass cultural programs, etc. to publicize and introduce them to the outside world. In the context of a community with a shared future for mankind, Nanjing is given priority to become a capital of peace blending Chinese excellent traditional culture with modern peace culture.

Conclusion

It was said that Nanjing was a city of a pathetic kind. The pain and suffering caused by the traumatic memories were deeply embedded in the urban collective memory, permeating the bricks and tiles of this city, and became an inseparable part of its memory. Therefore, in the early construction of urban memory, it was the consensus of the entire society to remember the history and learn from it. Academic research gradually evolved from the initial collection and display of responsive historical materials to a systematic scientific research on the truth of the history, intended to restore traumatic memories to the greatest extent, and avoided forgetting, distorting or tampering with these memories. The construction of memorial venues also restored and presented historical scenes from the perspective of the victims, exposed the cruelty of war, provided justice for the victims, spread and consolidated traumatic memories of the Nanjing Massacre, and greatly promoted the transformation of personal memories into collective and even national memories.

We also know that there are many ways to remember war trauma, depending on the audience's position and choice. It is also possible to build peace while not forgetting history and criticizing war. Gandhi once said, "An eye for an eye will only make the whole world blind." Trauma represents war and violence, which may keep people deep in fear and resentment of war when repeatedly emphasized. Consequently, hatred and violence will probably take root in the hearts of generations after generations and bring more violence. Thus, we need to change and transcend them. It is important to remember the tragic history, but it doesn't give much help to repair the war trauma through violence and revenge.

Constructing historical memory with the goal of gaining positive peace will free people from the negative influences of the past, and will also encourage ex-enemies to further repent and confess their crimes, and reconciliation will be made between different countries and even hostile countries. As time passes by, peace-building will create a hopeful and positive situation, where a new kind of interpersonal relationship will be created. Instead of repeatedly exposing the bloody historical scars, the study of peace emphasizes empathy, which may encourage others' resonation. When conflict occurs again, people will not choose anger, violence, and revenge for a second time, and peace and security will truly come. Of course, in peace-building, we still have many vital things to do such as cultivating kind-hearted emotions, critical thinking and empathy, to build an ecological environment in which man and nature coexist harmoniously, improve social fairness and justice, and reduce violence and discrimination in the society, etc. Only by sowing in peace and caring for it, can we reap a harvest of peace.

Nanjing is a city of peace today. Peace is not an illusory "fruit" any more, but a down-to-earth "process". In the new era, everyone can choose to be A PIECE OF PEACE, and build peace in thought and in action. Let all mankind stay away from the war and be bathed in the sunshine of peace and happiness, and this needs the joint efforts of you and me!

Main Bibliography

1. 贺云翱、周行道:《文化南京:历史与趋势》,南京:江苏人民出版社,2020年。

2. 经盛鸿:《南京沦陷八年史》(上、下),北京:社会科学文献出版社,2013年。

3. 李红涛、黄顺铭:《记忆的纹理:媒介、创伤与南京大屠杀》,北京:中国人民大学出版社,2017年。

4. 刘成:《和平学》,南京:南京出版社,2006年。

5. 刘成、[德]埃贡·施皮格尔:《全球化世界的和平建设——图解和平学》,北京:人民出版社,2015年。

6. 卢海鸣、杨新华:《南京民国建筑》,南京:南京大学出版社,2001年。

7. 谭志云:《南京教育小史》,南京:东南大学出版社,2011年。

8. 薛冰:《南京城市史》,南京:东南大学出版社,2015年。

9. 叶兆言:《南京传》,南京:译林出版社,2019年。

10. 章开沅:《南京大屠杀史料集4:美国传教士的日记与书信》,南京:江苏人民出版社、凤凰出版社,2005年。

11. 张生等:《南京大屠杀史研究(增订版)》(上、下),南京:凤凰出版社,2015年。

12. 张宪文:《南京大屠杀史料集》,南京:江苏人民出版社,2010年。

13. 赵德兴:《南京建城小史》,南京:东南大学出版社,2011年。

14. [英]安德鲁·瑞格比:《暴力之后的正义与和解》,刘成译,南京:译林出版社,2003年。

15. [美]大卫·巴拉什、查尔斯·韦伯:《积极和平——和平与冲突研究》,刘成等译,南京:南京出版社,2007年。

16. [法]莫里斯·哈布瓦赫:《论集体记忆》,毕然、郭金华译,上海:上海人民出版社,2002年。

17. [法]皮埃尔·诺拉:《记忆之场:法国国民意识的文化社会史》,黄艳红等译,南京:南京大学出版社,2015年。

18. [法]雅克·勒高夫:《历史与记忆》,方仁杰、倪复生译,北京:中国人民大学出版社,2010年。

19. [挪]约翰·加尔通:《和平论》,陈祖洲等译,南京:南京出版社,2006年。

20. [德]约翰·拉贝:《拉贝日记》,本书翻译组译,南京:江苏人民出版社、江苏教育出版社,2009年。

21. [美]约翰·W. 道尔:《拥抱战败:第二次世界大战后的日本》,胡博译,北京:生活·读书·新知三联书店,2015年。

22. Liu, Cheng, "A New Paradigm to Boost Right to Development for a Country", in China Society for Human Rights Studies, ed., Diversity of Civilizations and Development of World Human Rights, Beijing: China Intercontinental Press, 2021, pp.302-308.

23. Liu, Cheng, "A Single Spark Can Start a Prairie Fire: The Lonely Journey of Peace Studies in China", in Gerd-Bodo von Carlsburg and Annette Miriam Stroß, eds., (Non-) Educational Visions for the 21st Century: Humanities and Social Science Concepts after the End of the "Great" History of Mankind, Berlin: Peter Lang, 2021, pp.287-301.

24. Liu, Cheng, "Peace Studies of Asian Countries", in L. R. Kurtz, ed., Encyclopedia of Violence, Peace, and Conflict, Vol. 1, Academic Press, 2022, pp. 130-138.

25. Liu, Cheng and others, "Peace Education in China", in Kang Soon Won, Liu Cheng and others, Peace Education in Northeast Asia: A Situational Analysis, APCEIU, 2021, pp.28-66.

Afterword

On the day when the final draft was finished, the rainy season in Nanjing started as it does per annum. It was in the winter of 2017 that I began to write the book at the invitation of my supervisor, Professor Liu Cheng. At that time, he was planning for the series of "International Cities of Peace", so Nanjing was naturally to be included on the list. I gladly accepted his invitation, for I have followed him to promote peace studies in China for many years.

Though I have lived in Nanjing for several years, I felt that my understanding of her was far from enough after I actually started to write. What's more, during my writing, Nanjing is also undergoing changes over time, so I had to revise it again and again… I found that the closer I got to this city, the more I understood about her past and present, so her breadth and depth were more indescribable.

Professor Liu has been devoted much to promoting peace studies in China since 2001, and was appointed as the Chairholder of UNESCO Chair on Peace Studies at Nanjing University in 2017. He often says that this is a lonely road, as if one was walking alone in the sunset. The same was true for the writing of this book. Although it was written under Professor Liu's guidance, there have been already many historical and cultural books about Nanjing. Besides, I am just a world history teacher, and had little professional knowledge about

Nanjing, and only knew a little of peace studies. It made me feel so stressed and apprehensive to write a book about the first city of peace in China that the manuscript failed to meet Professor Liu's expectations many times. He remarked that we were not trying to write a historical work about Nanjing, but to reveal the core of this city—peace.

Only then did I realize that the writing should focus on "peace". This book talks about the history and the peace-building of Nanjing from the perspective of peace studies, which also serves as a part of her peace-building itself. I have studied under Professor Liu for many years, and have witnessed peace studies starting from scratch and growing up in China. I am greatly influenced by his persistence and his love for peace studies. So this book also embraces his interpretation of the history and future of Nanjing, as well as a record of his great efforts for the cause of peace studies in China.

In the course of writing, I also got much help from those, like Professor Jiang Shouming and Professor Hu Chuansheng; Ms. Xu Lei, editor-in-chief of the publishing house, Ms. Zheng Haiyan, assistant to the editor-in-chief, and Ms. Wang Yaqiong, editor-in-charge; Fan Haixiang, translator of the English version; picture providers, Wang Chun, Fang Fei, Ding Jie, Chen Xiangyu, Pang Hao, Song Renxiang, Luo Qingyun, Li Siqi, etc. I would also like to thank the Memorial Hall of the Victims in Nanjing Massacre by Japanese Invaders, the Nanjing Anti-Japanese Aviation Martyrs Memorial Hall, the Nanjing Non-Governmental Museum of War of Resistance against Japanese Aggression, Pearl S. Buck Memorial House at Nanjing University and other institutes for their support. Special thanks also go to my family members, for they were my loyal readers for every draft. I was moved by their selfless help. It is the common desire for peace that brings us together, and I know that the power of peace has always surrounded me.

As peace studies has taken root in China, it is believed that more and more people pay attention to the construction of Nanjing as an international city of peace, and more and more people give their eye teeth for a book to know something about the development of peace studies in China. It is hoped that through this book, the connection between Nanjing and peace will be tightened, and more people will be attracted to join in the peace-building.

I would like to dedicate this book to peace and pay tribute to every peace-loving activist!

Bai Shuang
August 2022

I was born and bred in Nanjing. My father went through that painful period of Nanjing. For this reason, he was full of hate for the Japanese. Before I worked, I had little knowledge of the Nanjing Massacre, because neither my parents nor my teachers would take the initiative to talk about that history. The author of this book, Bai Shuang, is a "new Nanjing citizen", who wrote this book from the perspective of an outsider. However, this did not impede her writing this book, because we have had sufficient understanding of the history of Nanjing, especially that traumatic history, in the course of our promoting peace studies in China.

This is a book that reviews the history of Nanjing from the perspective of peace. As historians, we all understand that history must be kept in mind, but we believe that pursuit of peace is the best option for memory and repair of traumatic history. We wrote this book based on this kind of thinking, so it may be different from others' writings about Nanjing. We hope that readers can appreciate and get more information about peace in Nanjing from this pamphlet, and support the construction of Nanjing into an international city of peace. We are sure that only in this way can the history of Nanjing be bridged with peace in the future, and be in consistence with that of the world.

We appreciate any demonstration and correction to the defects and mistakes in the book if any.

Liu Cheng
August 2022

For Photo Credits Please Refer to